D1591919

the
bay
rat
kid

the bay rat kid

GROWING UP IN OCEAN CITY, NEW JERSEY

1940s-1950s

by Jim Jeffries

First edition: October 2020.

Cover and book design by Mehran Azma.

Cover photos of the author from the Jeffries family collection.

ISBN 978-0-578-72533-8

Sandbar Publishing
125 Legendary Circle
Palm Beach Gardens, Florida 33418

Table of Contents

Nostalgia

The Free Dictionary describes the word "nostalgia" as:

"(1) A bittersweet longing for things, persons, or situations of the past.

(2) The condition of being homesick; homesickness."

The Cambridge Dictionary says it is:

"A feeling of pleasure and also slight sadness when you think about things that happened in the past:

- *Some people feel* nostalgia *for their schooldays.*
- *Hearing that song again filled him with* nostalgia.
- *a wave (= sudden strong feeling) of* nostalgia."

I never thought about this word until I got into the middle of writing this account of my youth and my Ocean City memories of that time. When I read these official definitions, they really hit home.

I'm sure we all can acknowledge that each of us has some form of this disease called nostalgia, which is one of the better ones to have. Fortunately, there is no cure for this malady, and maybe we don't want to find one.

"Nostalgia paints a smile on the stony face of the past." —Mason Cooley

"You're both suffering from acute nostalgia.
It's not life threatening, but I suggest you
spend a few weeks in Ocean City, New Jersey."

Early Thinking

As we age, it's normal to look back from time to time at our younger days as kids, remembering a variety of events and people. For me, growing up in Ocean City, New Jersey during the 1940s and 1950s was a very special time. Like most, I didn't realize back then how important those years would turn out to be. It seems the older I get, the more I search into the deepest part of my memory bank to recall as much as I can. I guess this sort of exercise can simply be thought of as an age thing, or another way of engaging in nostalgia.

My hope is that these little stories and photos that were a part of my life will spark memories of your own childhood experiences. The trick is, how much you can recall and in what detail. I will say that as I write, more things come to mind that I'd completely forgotten. If you find that the same mental phenomenon is true for you, give yourself a pat on the back as old memories become clear…finally.

"Back in the day" is a term we like to use in telling stories of our past. Children and grandchildren don't want to hear us say, "when I was your age," and neither did we when we were young. Let's just hope a few younger ones of today will be curious enough to read on.

First, let me say that nothing in my early life was much different or more special than yours or that of any other kid growing up in our little South Jersey seashore town, or anywhere else, for that matter. We just had different neighborhoods, addresses, friends, neighbors, time periods, relatives, and friends of relatives. No two childhoods are alike. And yet, the memories that we retain from childhood are what molded our lives forever. So this book is also about YOU and your memories, plus a little history.

Finally, these words are not intended to be a memoir, but I guess some of it is. This is not a novel; nor is it a diary. I don't even have actual "chapters"; I have "topics." The nerve of me. My exact age at the time of certain recollections is just a guess, and I often found it very difficult to put things in exact order as to years and events. Thus I bounce around a bit in this book, sometimes a lot, but I'm sure you will understand.

To verify my recollections, I had lots of help from excellent resources, including friends who also grew up in Ocean City. Any mistakes herein are my own.

Many good books have been written about Ocean City and its early days. This work intends to put a different and personal touch on a specific period of time, the 1940s and 1950s, via my memories. Included are a few old pictures and maybe some that you've never seen before.

You may have similar recollections of your own time growing up in Ocean City. Who knows; maybe I was even a small part of your past in some way.

What Got This Book Going Anyway?

In 2008, I started to create my family tree using the Ancestry.com program that many are familiar with today. To say that I got hooked on this project is an understatement. Not only have I done all sides of the Jeffries family, I've also created trees for my mother's family, my wife's, and several for friends. I'm hardly an expert but have learned enough to go back many generations and, in some cases, hundreds of years.

With the help of the wife of a distant relative I met online, we put together a book on The Jeffries Family, New Jersey. A copy is on file at The Ocean City Historical Museum. This 102-page document traces my family back to the early 1700s, when my ancestors came to America from England and ultimately ended up in Ocean City.

I recommend to everyone that you try to find your ancestors. It's fun, it's addictive, and it's good for the soul. In fact, creating my family tree led me to recall many childhood friends, neighbors, relatives, and experiences, which in turn inspired me to write this book. I trust the same will happen for you.

We all come from somewhere, as do our parents, grandparents, and far beyond. Finding those bloodlines is the challenge. And the adventure.

That's me, always walking toward the next adventure.

What Makes Us Who We Are?

Is it our DNA or what? Many of our personal building blocks seem to be based upon how we are raised, the people we get to know as youngsters, large and small events and experiences, and places we live in and visit. Probably a little of everything makes us who we are today.

Ever think about the relationships and circumstances that molded your life?

I always felt that kids who didn't grow up in Ocean City were at a disadvantage. Thus, one of the goals of this book is to point out the incredible time period that I and others near my age experienced in our little town of Ocean City, New Jersey. And yet, much of what I experienced could have happened anywhere in America.

Looking back, it seems like the 1940s and 1950s were the end of an era and the beginning of a new one. In the vast span of world history, this is nothing but a speck of time in the annals of the universe, but I love it.

The Greatest Generation

In my mind, those who lived, fought, and died during World War II, and those who went on after the war to build America as we know it today, were, in fact, the greatest, as Tom Brokaw wrote in his book *The Greatest Generation*. Looking back, I think that those of us who followed them were…

The Luckiest Generation

Postwar times were fortunate times for most of us growing up during this remarkable period, especially for those of us growing up in Ocean City. These two decades—starting in the 1940s and continuing in the 1950s—were full of tradition, patriotism, love of family, friends, and most important, our love for our city.

In a way, we were somewhat on the edge of being old fashioned and not quite reaching the modern age. We lived in older homes, second-floor apartments, cottages, and even garage apartments. Looking back, it seemed like the town was built one house at a time, with a couple of exceptions, one being the Merion Park neighborhood. I can't say I remember houses being razed simply to build new ones, as seems to be common practice today; in those days, buildings were torn down only when they were no longer salvageable.

Malls and strip malls of today weren't even an idea at the time, as we had Asbury Avenue. Walk into any store, and the shopkeeper or clerk greeted you by name. That sense of belonging also meant feeling safe pretty much everywhere; we were a mostly middle class city with hardly any crime to speak of. We never locked the front door and trusted everybody.

Perhaps that feeling of safety had to do with the fact that when I was born, Ocean City was essentially a small town. According to the Federal Census in 1940, which was two years after I was born, the population was 4,676. Today the population is about triple that figure. The summer numbers were then, and still are today, much higher.

Roots

As hard as some of us may try, we never forget our roots. Even today when I'm asked, "Where are you from?" I always say "Ocean City," even though my first 20 years were in the city, and the next 61, not too far away. Many of you who hold your hometown close to your heart may say something similar.

Roots are more than family and the location where we were born. They are also the people we meet along the way, the people who had an impact, sometimes a hidden impact, on our young lives. We all go through this mysterious segment of life's journey one way or another, and we never forget the people who helped us through it.

I hope I have you thinking about this beginning process in your life. I also hope that as you read through these pages, you can picture in your own mind your personal experiences with the people who had an impact on your life, regardless of where your own "Ocean City" was located. Yes, I'm encouraging you to be nostalgic, which is not a crime, at least not yet.

Toward the end of this book, I have asked a few old friends to make a brief comment on this era, plus I have listed many of the events, breakthroughs, and inventions of the 1940s and 1950s that you will recognize. All of us have reason to marvel at what has happened in our lifetime and particularly in this era of:

The Luckiest Generation: The 1940s and 1950s, in Ocean City, New Jersey.

Just A Little Background

As best as I can determine, my family came to America in the early 1700's from England to New England, then to southern New Jersey in the Absecon, Egg Harbor Township, Atlantic City area, in the early 1800s. Then, around 1882 or possibly earlier, my great-grandfather John B. Jeffries brought his large family from Atlantic City to Ocean City, which was roughly four years after the official founding of our city. The rest, as they say, is history.

I've often wondered what motivated my great-grandfather John B's decision to move the family to Ocean City. How did they travel? Did they come from Atlantic City by boat, horse and buggy, or what? Was John B dreaming of a better life in coming to this start-up city with his wife and nine children? I also wonder how he found a place to live, got his first job in a new city, or figured out where to purchase food. History books don't typically answer such basic questions we have about our ancestors, and I can tell you that John B left no clues or diaries. He was just a laborer, and we are left to use the best of our imagination.

If you're wondering what Ocean City was like back then, records from 1882 indicate that 400 people or less made up the local population, and there were 178 structures, which included 112 homes. Seven years later, in 1890, the official population was 452. Amazing to me is that possibly seven or more of those 452 residents were ancestors of mine. Of course that is just a wild guess, but it's fun to speculate.

By the time my great-grandfather John B arrived in Ocean City with his wife Lovina and their children, including 12-year-old George, my grandfather, much of the city had been laid out, and development had been underway for some time. Which I hope meant ample work opportunities for John B, who was listed in federal census reports as a "laborer" or "bayman."

In John B's new home town, his son George, my grandfather, also became a bayman, laborer, boat captain, and a lather. "Lath and plaster" was the method of creating interior walls and ceilings long before sheetrock came onto the building scene.

My guess is that George worked on many of the early structures in Ocean City from the 1890's and for many years thereafter. Grandpop was a volunteer fireman and also secretary to the Ocean City Liberty Fire Company #3, and he probably attended Ocean City School, which was built in 1882 and was the first school in the city.

Liberty Firehouse. Courtesy of the Ocean City Fire Department and Ryan Scharff, OCFD Historian. The close-up of the man in the inset image is my grandfather George Jeffries.

As for my great-grandfather John B, I have not found information indicating that he was anything other than a laborer, bayman, boat captain, and possibly a volunteer fireman. The only scrap of evidence I have about his life, other than federal census reports, was a small, barely legible 1905 clipping from the *Ocean City Sentinel* when he died. It says:

Fatally stricken on Street April 12

John B. Jeffries, aged 72 years, one of the pioneer residents of this city, died this morning. He was fatally ill on the street.

When I found this tiny piece of newspaper in an envelope, I thought I had found King Tut's Tomb. The phrase, "one of the pioneer residents," appeals to the pride I have in my family and my Ocean City heritage.

For years, the family homestead was at 304-306 9th Street. It was a small, two-family structure that was razed some time ago, but I remember when my uncle George Jeffries (youngest son of my grandfather George Jeffries) and his family lived there. The family had occupied both sides of the dwelling for years; however, according to the 1894 *Ocean City Guide*, my grandfather George, his brother John H, and my great-grandfather John B lived at 347 West Avenue. All three listed their occupations at the time as "captain," which I understand to mean boat captain.

My grandfather George Jeffries died in 1943 when I was only five years of age, and I do not have any recollection of him. Actually, I never knew any of my grandparents on either side.

My father, Leroy Jeffries, was born in 1895, the first of six children. At the age of 12, he worked at a grocery store close to where he lived. In 1919, after serving in World War I, he purchased the Ocean City Market House at 860 Asbury Avenue from his former employer, Mr. Furman Willis, and owned it for about 16 years until he was appointed Ocean City's postmaster in 1935. More on Pop later.

Here's Grandpop George Jeffries holding my big sister, Annetta.

Setting The Stage

I was born in the early fall of 1938, in Somers Point at the Atlantic Shores Hospital & Sanitarium, which was established in 1928. In 1939, it became Shore Memorial Hospital, the same place where most, if not all, of my cousins and friends were also born.

My sister, Annetta, was eight years older than I, and my brother, Bill, was just five years older. I know that my father and his siblings were all born in Ocean City, probably at home, rather than in a hospital.

(L) Our family home at 1116 Bay, as it looked back in the day. (R) My uncle John Svit.

We lived at 1116 Bay Avenue, a house built in 1923 by my Uncle John Svit, who lived next door at 1118 Bay, in a similar house now owned by Steve and Mary Ann Gring. Our house was one of three houses on our block that Uncle John built in the 1920s, and believe it or not, all of these homes remain pretty much the same as they were back then.

That's a miracle in this town!

My oldest cousin, Margaret Svit, was born in 1918. Our youngest cousin, Rosemary Jeffries, wasn't born until 1949, which makes for about a 30-year span for 14 cousins. One aunt became a Moncrief, another familiar name in town. Yes, Marlene Moncrief Murphy's Uncle Bill Moncrief married my Aunt Edith Jeffries. Does that make us kissin' cousins? Who knows?

Mom, known to all as Florence, was born in Atlantic City in 1900. She was an incredible person, a great homemaker, and an old fashioned stay-at-home mom. More on Mom later.

Mom and Pop in front of our family home.

Those Very Early Years

Let's face it; most of us have little, if any, memories of our lives before we were four or five years of age, certainly nothing of great importance. Plus, wouldn't you agree that we all have a hard time trying to remember what age we were when we do recall something? This was my biggest challenge in writing these accounts. With this in mind, for most of this book I'll be covering a period of about 15 years of memories, from around 1944, when I was six years old, to 1959, when I was 21.

Sittin' on the dock of the bay was always a favorite thing to do, as far back as I can remember.

The Real Start

My earliest memory from age five is still clear to me. It was the first day of kindergarten at Central Avenue School. I can describe the dress my mother had on as she walked me to school on that eventful day. Some might think it weird to be able to remember something like that, but I do. It was a dark brown dress with white polka dots. Mom would have been 43 at the time.

When I attended Central Avenue School, it was only a K-6 school. In my father's day, it was also a high school, from which Pop graduated in 1912. When he went to grammar school, it was at Ocean City School, which was built in 1882 and taken down in 1906. In its place, and on the same property, the city built Central Avenue School.

While Central Ave School was being built, the students were schooled in four different temporary buildings: The Bourse Building, Trower's Hall, Champion's Store, and the Music Pavilion. This is useless trivia, but now you know, in case anyone asks you.

In my very first days of kindergarten, I remember getting what I assumed were physicals or checkups. Yep, boys and girls all lined up in just our underwear, one by one, waiting to be looked at by the school doctor. I don't think they do that anymore. I also wonder if any of my old classmates remember this event.

Our teacher was Miss Shaw, later to become Mrs. Chew. Old schools like this had so-called "cloak rooms," but I don't remember having any cloaks; just woolen hats, coats, mittens, galoshes, scarves, and big hooks to hang stuff on. The dress code was wear whatever you owned, even if was a hand-me-down.

Mr. Brennan was the school janitor. Part of his job was to keep the heat going during the winter with several large, coal-fired steam boilers, though regulating the heat evenly throughout the building was impossible, especially during the spring and fall when the weather changed so much outside.

Seeing the coal truck in the alley delivering coal down a chute got our attention, especially because Mr. Brennan enjoyed showing us the burning coals when he opened the door to feed in more coal. We could feel the heat coming out of the opened door, which was somewhat of a learning experience.

As for the warmer months, the words "air conditioning" weren't invented yet, at least not in our schools. We just had big heavy windows to open and close.

Another memorable part of school life was cleaning the blackboard erasers. It was a big deal if the teacher chose you to stick your hands out of the window and clap the erasers together. Sometimes the chalk dust blew back in your face. Who remembers that one?

Then there were the play yards. The south side play yard was for girls, the north side for boys, both totally covered with concrete. I can't imagine the next-door neighbors being happy with the schoolyard noise of us kids screaming and yelling, but we all loved it. Of course we lined up by class when it was time to go inside. I imagine this process probably hasn't changed much over the years.

I would say that we had the last of the old wooden desks with inkwells and flip-up tops. I always thought they were as old as the school itself. Somehow they were connected together. I sort of remember them being replaced by a slightly more "modern" design, at least by the standards of the day.

I think about all the good memories that so many of us over the years have of this school. This is where new friendships began that were outside of our immediate neighborhood.

Today, the building that used to be my grammar school is the police department. I commend the city for not subjecting our old school to the wrecking ball. I've also often wondered how many police officers were once students at Central Avenue and later served in the police department in this same building. There must be a few out there.

Officer Tim Harris, AKA Big Tim

Affectionately known as "Big Tim," this police officer was a local fixture of long standing, especially with young children crossing the street at 9th and Asbury Avenue. His teddy-bear persona was just what we needed in our early years going to Central Avenue School.

Every day we would run into his waiting arms, each of us hoping he would pick us up first, then take our hands to cross the street. We were lucky; kids from other parts of town didn't get to have personal contact with this remarkable man.

Officer Harris would always have some encouraging words for us: "Do good in school today" or "Listen to your teacher." At times he would remind me he knew my father, the postmaster. Maybe that little reminder made me behave.

Tim Harris lived on Pleasure Avenue, between 6th & 7th Streets, and was a larger-than-life figure who walked his beat up and down Asbury Avenue for many years. How many remember him?

Officer Tim Harris, also known as Big Tim. With the kind permission of the Ocean City Historical Museum.

First Friendships

Your first friends are generally the ones that live closest to you, and as you grow older you simply gain more. One of my earliest friends was Chick Kisby. The Kisbys lived on the corner of Walton Place and Bay Avenue, a block north of me. Chick's father worked for Atlantic City Electric Company, and during the Second World War one of his jobs was to paint the tops of street lights black so that they couldn't be seen from the ocean. The Kisbys owned a car, and I could count on Mrs. Kisby to drive us to school if it was raining out. (I missed being able to take the school bus by half a block, as you had to live south of 12th Street. Now that just wasn't fair.)

Chick and I were in the same class from K-12 and were also close playmates, particularly when we were old enough to cross 11th Street by ourselves. We played on Walton Place, which was a dead-end street and a safe place to ride our bikes: Nothing like a dead end street to play in. We also played in the weeds on 11th Street, near the bay, where 21 W. 11th Street now sits and the two houses on either side of it.

My sister, Annetta, and I.

Cousin Donald and I, in our pre-fort period.

Just Little Kids

I was three months older than my cousin Donald Svit, who lived next door. We were kept pretty close to home as little guys and played together as kids do. His father, my Uncle John, was a local builder and built us a sandbox. Thanks to Uncle John, Donald also probably had the biggest swing in town.

Donald and I played cowboys and Indians or cops and robbers, and we fought over who would get to be Roy Rogers or Gene Autry, who were the most popular movie-star cowboys of my youth. They were our heroes, and we loved pretending to be them.

We also played at being firemen putting out imaginary fires down the dirt alley or on a boat behind us. I think all little boys want to be firemen, regardless of when they were born.

Plus we built forts, a childhood event that I'm not sure happens much anymore. We would drag pieces of wood that we got from Uncle John's shop or that were just lying around in the boatyard and build ourselves a little structure with a door. Most of our forts were just big enough for a couple of kids to play in, but to us they were palaces. One time we did make the most out of an old abandoned wooden boat and called it our fort, but it was really just an old boat that had had its day and which took over our imagination.

Forts, Weeds, And Cigarettes

One of our forts was in the weeds on the north side of 11th Street near the bay, which I consider the neighborhood. One day, a kid who will remain anonymous came by with a pack of Camels. He was a little older, he knew how to smoke, and he was rather cocky about it.

Anyway, he tried to teach me how to inhale, as I could only puff and only managed to do that a couple of times. I just couldn't get the hang of it and managed to get sick, which scared the hell out of me. That was the last time I tried to smoke. Since then, when anyone asks me if I ever smoked, I always say, "I quit when I was 11."

To which my wife says, "That's a stale joke."

Growing Up Too Fast

When Cousin Donald and I were 10 years old, his father, my uncle John, died. Uncle John was the first dead person I saw, laid out at the Smith Funeral Home on Central Avenue, now Godfrey Funeral Home. You just don't forget a scene like this at that age, an eerie memory in a way. Mom never warned me about what I was about to see.

We all have one of these first-time life events that sticks in your mind forever. This was mine. Maybe you had a similar experience at a young age also.

Several years later, Aunt Helen Svit sold the house, the boathouse on the bay, and moved into a smaller house on Simpson Avenue. Her son Jack kept Uncle John's large workshop by the alley. As for my cousin Donald, he never seemed to have grown up in the normal fashion; he didn't graduate high school, and he continued living at home with his mother.

At one point I learned that Donald worked for motel owner Al Kazmarck, fixing his rental bikes at the motel at 9th & Wesley and doing other odd jobs around town. I'm sure there might be a few people from Ocean City who remember him.

Donald died at age 39, two years after his mother passed. Although I had little contact with Donald for a long time after I left town, we had been inseparable for the first 12 years or so of our lives.

This sort of thing happens within all families, maybe yours too.

Out Of The Neighborhood

My friends from the 34th Street area were Dave & George Loder, John Carew, and Dewey Powell. With the exception of the airport, the city dump, and the old incinerator, there wasn't much of anything from about 20th Street to 34th Street, except meadows and bayberry bushes that ran just a few feet from Bay Avenue. This was the perfect spot for a fort; the bayberry bushes and weeds were a little higher than we were and made good cover.

We built a neat fort there, fit for a king, and I would estimate that it was about a block or so south of where Holy Trinity Episcopal Church stands today. This fort was so big that we actually had rooms, plus a large cherry tree in the middle. We were in heaven.

On the north side of the airport was a defunct development from the 1930's called Riviera. City blocks had been laid out, and some curbing had been installed, but there were just dirt streets there. It was a great place to ride our bikes.

Today, this area of Ocean City is no longer the wilderness it was to us kids in the early 1950s. There are now man-made lagoons, new streets, and many high-end houses here, and when I finally revisited this part of town after all the changes, it was a real eye opener.

I understand that all the dirt that was removed to create the lagoons was deposited in other marshland areas nearby to create more development. These other marshland areas would generally be the areas between Haven Avenue (railroad tracks) and Bay Avenue, from about 16th Street south to 34th Street, with just a few houses. The Stainton Preserve as you know it today is what the entire section looked like for years. The other developed area that received the dirt was from the airport south to 34th Street.

This was an enormous transfer of dirt from one area to another. Obviously this also amounted to a tremendous loss of marshland, but there are winners and losers in this modern-day era of expansion and development.

When the weather was too cold for exploring outside the neighborhood, playing in the snow with my brother, Bill, was just as much fun.

The War Years—WWII

Many who are around my age and therefore were maybe five to seven years of age or older during World War II have a few memories, sometimes vague ones, of those war years. Not about the war itself, but about things that happened around us. I trust you may have some too, if you're old enough.

Here are a few from a year or so before the end of the war that stayed with me.

I was too young to join the Navy, but that didn't stop Mom from fitting me up as a little sailor.

Tin Cans

Crushing empty tin cans, which actually weren't tin, with your feet and rolling up aluminum foil into big balls were little things that everyone did to help the war effort. We got the aluminum foil by stripping it from chewing gum wrappers or cigarette packs. I'm not sure where the empty cigarette packs came from, as no one smoked at home. Scrap metal collection was important too.

I would guess this was the beginning of residential recycling as we know it today. *The Sentinel-Ledger* had an article entitled "SCRAPS from the Scrap," which was about a citywide program to support the war effort by doing these little exercises. It may not sound like a lot, but when you figure people from towns all across the nation were doing things like this at the time, I'm sure it all made a difference.

The Tower

Sometime in the 1920's, my father had been Post Commander of the American Legion. In 1941 he was part of a group that the American Legion organized, and which consisted of around 500 volunteers who manned what we all called "The Tower," a lookout structure built on top of the Music Pier. I seem to remember that Pop had an armband to that effect. Known as "spotters," Pop and his fellow volunteers took shifts looking for German U-Boats or anything suspicious out in the ocean.

Officially, The Tower was called the Ocean City WWII Aircraft Observation Tower and was part of the Aircraft Warning Service. I remember Pop taking me and my brother up to that very tower. I couldn't have been more than six or so, but I remember climbing up a ladder or steep steps to enter that special small observation room that looked far over the ocean.

Of course, I was too young to understand what it was used for, but it surely was important for our shoreline defense.

I'm sure there are at least a few of us left who recall this wartime tower. Maybe you went up inside of it too? I know that Marla Adams, a friend and classmate, got to see it when her father took her up there. (A trivia side note: Marla later became an actress and was on *The Young and the Restless* for many years.)

When the war ended, the need for The Tower ended. It was finally removed during reconstruction work on the Music Pier in 1982, following extensive storm damage.

The Tower and Music Pier, Ocean City, 1961.

Gooey Stuff, Yuck

When you went to the beach, it was very possible to step on "tar balls," which were globs of fuel oil from ships that had been torpedoed and sunk out in the ocean. I remember Mom cleaning my feet constantly with something from a small bottle she kept in her beach bag, kerosene I think. "Watch where you walk," was her frequent warning. Most people were always looking down and side-stepping a glob of tar or more.

I'm sure many of you have personal memories of this, as tar balls continued to wash up for some time, even after the war.

Blackouts

The whole idea of deliberate blackouts was to reduce or eliminate any light that might help German U-Boats spot the shoreline, though as a young child it was something I didn't quite understand.

The top half of headlights on cars were painted black to reduce their light. Light poles that faced the ocean were also blackened out. Sometimes we had to cover all the windows with bed sheets on our enclosed front porch. I don't know why, as we lived on Bay Avenue, and I don't think enemy ships could spot us that far away. Go figure.

Look Up

Another common sight was seeing blimps or dirigibles fly up and down the beach. Their job was of course to look for enemy craft of any kind. We would constantly wave to the crew as they flew by. The whole defensive system was a coordinated effort up and down the Jersey Shore, town by town as well as on both the entire east and west coasts.

The Moyer Company

When war came, The Moyer Company, later to become Moyer & Son, was a major player with the military in building various types of small support boats.

If you now live in the area of 20th to 22nd Street and the bay, chances are that your house or your neighbor's sits where Moyer's large boat-building facility was once located. Just prior to the war, Joe Moyer was building boats at 312 Bay Avenue, then between 8th and 9th Streets on the bay. In November of 1942, having won a number of U.S. Army contracts, Moyer leased city-owned property between 22nd & 23rd and the bay to expand his wartime operation dramatically, even though the property was zoned for residential use.

All I remember was Pop driving us down this dirt road, and suddenly we saw this gigantic building, a huge Quonset hut. The dirt road was Texas Avenue, which was eliminated years later, when the lagoons were created in that area. I recall we never got out of the car, but I'm sure Pop wanted to show us where his two brothers, my uncles, worked at building boats for the war. It was these very boats that I saw travelling behind our house on the bay, on their way to some unknown destination. I didn't figure that out until years later, but I sure remember watching these convoys of boats heading north. Somehow we learned that they were on the way, as many would line the docks to witness this parade of military watercraft.

Of course, when the war ended, the government contract work at Moyer's ended, and so did his ability to stay at that city-owned location. After the war, Moyer wanted the city to change the zoning to light industry so that he could remain in business there. In the end, the city didn't move on that idea, the buildings were taken down, and Moyer relocated his operation to Linwood, where he built pre-fabricated homes.

Note: For more about The Moyer Company, You can visit the Ocean City Historical Museum website at OCNJmuseum.org. There you can find all the issues of *The Binnacle* for 2018 and 2019. The Fall Issue 2018 #24, written by William Pehlert on The Moyer Company, is great reading and includes many photographs.

(L) Six of the WWII-era boats that Moyer's built. (R) Here's Moyer's Quonset hut, the hub of boat-building activities. Both photos provided with the kind permission of the Ocean City Historical Museum.

Holtz Boat Works

During the war, Holtz Boat Works and Basin, which was located at 8th Street and the bay, was also a key player in the marine life of the city. Holtz contracted with the U.S. military to build a number of very large barges that were later used in the D-Day Landing at Normandy. I do not remember seeing any of these barges or other military crafts but am thankful we can see photos of them today.

Following the war, Holtz did extensive work for Chris Montagna on the many boats that Chris ran from his very own Chris's Seafood Restaurant. I vividly recall seeing The Flying Pony boat, The Flying Saucer boat, and others being built or worked on at Holtz Boat Works. Several were converted PT boats. Riding my bike to this facility to watch them work on these boats was, for me, an adventure. I just couldn't get enough of it.

At one point, the Holtz property took up the entire block from 7th to 8th Streets on the bay. However, Holtz Boat Works and the whole block were eventually sold and replaced with condos and a few single-family homes.

(L) One of the many military barges that Holtz Boat Works built. With the kind permission of the Ocean City Historical Museum. (R) Chris Montagna's speedboat, The Flying Pony. Courtesy of Frank Esposito.

Final War Thoughts

Although I was too young back then to realize that a war was going on, let alone a world war, I do recall going to The Village Theater and seeing newsreels of actual war coverage. Nevertheless, I was just too young to understand what I was seeing. That understanding would follow in the years to come.

Ocean City did its fair share in contributing to the war effort, as did every small and large town in the United States, from supplying men and women in uniform, to building necessary equipment and arms and, in our case, protecting our shoreline and building military watercraft and barges.

Although this is a book about Ocean City personal memories, yours and mine, we must remember those Ocean City citizens who served and, in some cases, died in service to our country. In one of his many books, Ocean City historic writer Fred Miller cites these numbers:

"In World War I, 223 men from Ocean City registered for the draft, and 5 were killed. In World War II, 491 men and women from Ocean City served, and 34 were killed."

Please think about that, and please visit the war memorial monuments located between 5th and 6th on Wesley Avenue. These monuments list all of their names; you may recognize some of them. One would be Leroy Jeffries on the WWI monument. Originally, this monument stood on the corner of 9th and Asbury Ave at City Hall, near the water fountain.

Our Neighborhood

The 1100 block on Bay Avenue was the best, at least to me. Only a dirt alley separated the back of our house and the boatyards on the bay. We didn't have any summer residents like other parts of town. We were all locals.

As with many other memories, you simply don't forget what your immediate neighborhood looked liked. I'm sure you could also draw a map of the block where you grew up. If you don't think you can, try it. If you don't think I can, read on.

To give you a better picture of this block at that time, I've made an effort to re-create the layout. Please forgive me if I don't have things exactly correct, but it's the best I could do. As you read on, you may need to refer back to the map to get a clear picture of the layout of the block.

Hand-drawn map of my childhood street, which back then was the center of my world.

Outback

"Outback" (not the restaurant) was where I often told Mom I was going. Not across the street or next door, but "outback." The term meant any of the three boatyards, boathouse, or docks. "Outback," which was my play yard, took up the entire block on the bay front, and Mom always knew about where I was. Sometimes she sent my brother or sister to check on me or call me to dinner; other times she came looking for me herself. Typically, it was hard to get me home. I once recall someone calling me a "bay rat." I confess that was a good description of me at the time.

By the way, my brother, Bill, did many similar things that I did in the boatyards and neighborhood. Five years seems like a huge difference in our ages, but watching him work on boats at times is what this little brother remembers. So these stories and memories could have easily been his too.

The Three Boatyards

Behind our house were three boatyards. Cappy Wright's was the one directly behind us and where I spent most of my time. Next to Uncle John's boathouse, on the south side, was Bart Turner's yard, later to become Hallamarine, which ran from Bay Avenue to the bay. Uncle John's property ran from 1118 Bay Avenue all the way to his boathouse on the bay between Cappy's and Turner's.

Adjacent to Turner's on the south side was May's Boatyard and Basin, which also ran from Bay Avenue to the bay and bordered on 12th Street on both sides. A simple dirt road from Bay Avenue to the bay separated Turner's and May's.

As a kid, I couldn't wait to help launch boats in the spring and haul them out in the fall at all three boatyards, but mostly at Cappy's. Each boatyard had a similar railway system for launching boats. No mechanical lifts like they have today, though Turner's/Hallamarine, eventually had an earlier style of lift in the late 50s, as did May's. At the time, all boats were built of wood, but fiberglass ones were on the horizon. I do remember one that was made of steel.

The launch process was an interesting one. It consisted of using the brute strength of those who were around to help roll or push a boat on two-inch rollers from its winter storage space over to the "cradle," which was positioned on the railway. Once the boat was sitting on the cradle, it was eased down into the water by pushing it by hand as the cables were carefully loosened. Oftentimes the boat owners were present to lend a hand or just nervously watch their pride and joy roll down the railway to the water.

The reverse process happened in the fall.

Every launch or takeout was not only a happening, but also a labor-intensive job that was carried out like a symphony, most of the time. There was some planning needed when the yard would launch or haul out a boat, because eight to ten boats sat in a row during winter storage. The first boat hauled out for the winter would be the last one launched in the spring. The last boat hauled out in the winter would be the first one launched in the spring.

A system of cables and an old winch were used to control the launch and haul out boats when they were sitting on the cradle. I knew something was happening at Cappy's when I could hear them starting up the gas-operated winch, which had a very distinctive noise and was a relic in itself at the time. That poor winch struggled when hauling out bigger and heavier boats.

Sometimes the cables snapped. "LOOK OUT!" roared the cry as the boat and cradle slid back, uncontrolled, into the water. Once in a while, the cradle would derail in the water, which resulted in a string of cuss words. Had my mother heard this language, I would have been banned from the yard.

I was the boy in the yards they would use when needed to retrieve a tool or whatever that may have dropped to the bottom of the hull or bilge. Or they'd have me run to the shop to get something. I was skinny, little, and could go anywhere.

I was never hired or paid for anything, though once in a while I was slipped a few dollar bills. I was just there watching and gladly pitched in to help, even when I wasn't asked to. Fortunately, I don't remember ever getting hurt. I do wish I could remember some of the boatyard jargon of the day. Maybe it will come back to me.

Photographs of these boatyards are extremely hard to come by. It seems the beach, boardwalk, and old hotels had the greatest attraction for photographers during that era and in earlier years. I guess boatyards were never thought of as being picturesque.

Every kid has a place to play in; where was yours? It might have been the boardwalk, under the boardwalk, or it may have been a vacant lot or some other attraction that you and your friends considered your playground. The boatyards were mine.

Cappy's Boatyard

P art of Cappy's Boatyard included a very large shop used to build and repair various sized boats. Inside the shop was every woodworking tool and machine you could imagine, but there was one process that always fascinated me. I don't think this process had a name, but I'll paint a picture for you.

Ever wonder how boat builders would get plank of wood shaped to fit the curvature of the hull on a boat? Here's how I learned the process at Cappy's.

First you have about a 10-foot piece of cast iron pipe, maybe 8" wide. This pipe is set up on a frame at about a 25-degree angle, with a flame at the bottom to heat up a small amount of water that was poured inside to the closed end at the bottom.

My sister, Annetta, with a view of Cappy's Boatyard in the background.

The heat would bring the water to a boil, then to steam. The plank would be placed into the pipe and the steam over a period of time to loosen up the fibers of the wood. Then the magic would begin.

At the proper time, they removed the plank from the pipe and immediately secured it with clamps and screwed it to the ribs of the hull being built. The board seemed to become like a piece of a soft chewing gum stick. To this little kid, it was magic.

Interestingly, our wooden lifeguard boats were repaired this way for years when they suffered some sort of damage. This system of bending planks was probably used for hundreds of years around the world and probably still is today, especially for those restoring old wooden boats.

Another marine process was "caulking," but not the kind that comes out of a tube. Wooden boats needed to be caulked at times when leaks occurred. They would take a strip of cotton from a roll and drive the cotton between the planks on the hull with a dull, chisel-type tool called a caulking iron.

The next step would be to fill part of the bilge with water to the necessary level. The water would begin to drip through the hull, but the cotton and wood fibers would swell up, and the leaking would come to a stop. Over the life of the boat, re-caulking would need to be done from time to time to stop or avoid further leaks. Now you know.

For me, this was a real learning experience, though it was but a simple method in the building and maintenance of a wooden boat. Hearing the loud clinking sound of a hammer hitting the dull-edged tool was a distinctive noise, and I knew then they were fixing a leak. This was a signal for me to go and watch.

I was about 11 when Cappy Wright died in 1949 at the age of 72. Two new guys took over the operation, one whose name I think was Rowland, and the other was Russ Adams, who built a large number of Garveys, which were small, flat-nosed boats, in the shop. Russ was the brother of T. Lee Adams, one of my favorite outback friends. Anyhow, I was there to help them, just like I'd helped Cappy.

I believe the next operator to take over the yard was my friend Frank Esposito's Uncle Tony Capezza, though I never got to know him. The actual owner of this boatyard that had once been Cappy's was Dr. John Whitaker, a prominent local physician for many years, who also owned Hogates' Restaurant and Ocean City Golf Course in Somers Point. He lived in the cottage on the bay at 11th Street, which had a small gas dock in front where I pumped gas when I was a little older.

Handing the gas hose down to the boat owner when the water was choppy could be a real challenge at times.

Once in a while, the guys at this boatyard let me help paint the bottom of boats with "copper paint" just before they were launched. The function of this paint is something that I never figured out. Why would they launch a boat with wet paint on it? This was a thick, reddish-brown paint that got all over you if you weren't careful. Mom had the unpleasant chore of cleaning me up afterwards and wasn't very happy about it. One time she made me take off all my clothes, which was embarrassing for me at the time.

In the winter, the boats were stored up to the alley about 15 feet from our back fence. A few older ones never left their spot. The view from my back bedroom of all these boats waiting to be launched in the spring never got stale.

Bart Turner's Yard

Mr. Turner lived at 7 West 11th Street, behind DeHart's Grocery Store, a very short drive in his pickup truck to his business, which was called Bart Turner's Yard (and later became Hallamarine). Mr. Turner only had the one shop, which was accessible from Bay Avenue and was next to the bulkhead. For the most part, Mr. Turner operated his yard pretty much as Cappy's did, except that Turner's did not do any boat building or major woodwork. Turner's seemed to do more engine work and general repairs in addition to boat storage, but only had a few slips for rental.

My clearest memory of Turner's is when they worked on Chris Craft speed boats. These mahogany boats were the rage at the time and always drew many onlookers. Many of these boats can be seen today at vintage classic boat shows, one of which is held in Tuckerton each year. Restored, they are worth many times their original cost.

To this day, mahogany boats always get my attention. When I see these refurbished works of art, they continue to bring back memories for me, and I'm sure they do the same for many others, just like antique and classic cars do.

The building with the peaked roof, on the left, by the water, is the original Bart Turner's Yard. Hallamarine took over in the late 1950s, renamed the place, and added the buildings on the right side.

May's Boatyard and Basin

May's was owned by Mr. Ed May and later by his two sons, Ed Jr. and Gordon, all of whom I remember well. Mr. May started his business in 1934, and the property was sold in 1979. It was definitely a family operation.

Like the other boatyards, May's had a similar railway system with a winch. The family's house was also a store, which was on the south side of 12th and the bay. Renting row boats and selling bait and fishing gear was their niche in the area, plus storage and service for boats, as well as a gas dock.

One of my memories of Mr. May was his kindness to me and my friend Billy Blevin, who lived opposite Chris's Seafood Restaurant on Palen Avenue. A fun thing that Billy and I did was setting "minnie traps" (for those of you who don't fish, minnies are minnows), and Mr. May would let us use one of his row boats to do that. We would row across to the meadows, set our traps, return the next day, get our catch, and sell it to Mr. May for bait. I think Mr. May gave us $1.00 for a bucket full of minnows without water. He would remind us that we could use the boat "free of charge," but only when we were bringing him minnies. Though Billy and I didn't realize it at the time, it was a good experience for two kids learning about America's free enterprise system.

Many years later, I learned that up north on the Jersey shore, minnows are called "killies." Who created that confusion?

May's property was divided by the city-owned 12th Street Pavilion, which was located at the end of the street. The 12th Street Pavilion was one of the few places on the bay where the public could sit and enjoy the sight of the bay and passing pleasure boats. They could also watch us kids dive, jump, and swim off the dock.

There was another similar pavilion at 14th and the bay, but unfortunately it no longer exists. Some people would bring their rod and reel and fish from the pavilion.

In my mind, most of the boat owners from all three yards were rich guys from Philadelphia. The fact is that they were all very nice people and friendly to me. I got to know many of them and their boats by name, and they got to know me.

Aerial view of May's operation with 12th Street Pavilion in the middle. Courtesy of Ed May, Jr.

There is no doubt that I probably drove them crazy with questions, as kids my age could do, but I always showed a willingness to help them do anything, even going to the corner store for a pack of Camels. Mr. Goldy, the owner of the corner store, wanted to know who the cigarettes were for. I had to go back and get a note the first time, but after that, no problem.

I also remember a Mr. Lewis who tried to explain the stock market to me, using a stick and drawing lines in the dirt by his boat in storage. I honestly can't say

I understood the lesson, and it was probably the last time I asked someone in the boatyard what they did to make money. I just didn't understand that it was none of my business. This setting would have been perfect for a Norman Rockwell painting, which leads me into the next subject.

May's Boatyard and Basin, street view.

Marine ads from this era. Courtesy of Steve Warnalis.

Boatyard Art

Although I never went to an art museum or anything of the sort when I was a boy, the boatyards were popular places for artists to come and paint the old boats and docks. I would watch them set up their easels and brushes, then paint their subjects. This was probably my first experience in watching the art world first hand. I just didn't understand that each one of these people had a gift, and I wondered why I couldn't paint like them.

One lady gave me a tablet and told me to "draw what I see and see what I draw." I still remember her words coming from under her floppy straw hat, but I failed her instructions.

I have often wondered where some of those artists' paintings ended up. Probably in somebody's attic. One artist was Mr. Tony Pileggi, Don Pileggi's uncle, who was really a sign letterer. His business in town was lettering boat names on the sterns of boats, plus trucks, and he even lettered the lifeguard boats for the city. I was amazed at his steady hand and talent. This quiet man would chat with you as he worked. It was clearly a learning experience that I vividly remember. To me, he was the first artist I ever knew.

From Oars to Outboards

In 1907, Mr. Ole Evinrude invented the first outboard motor. This Norwegian-American from Wisconsin began a whole new mode of boat propulsion, which grew into a massive industry that continues today. Over the years, more manufacturers with newer and bigger models came into prominence.

Outboard motors played a significant part in the landing of troops at D-Day, and after the war, this industry took off. I'm not sure when it started, but I recall that at some point May's and other row boat rental marinas began to rent row boats with small outboard motors. Each yard had a 55-gallon barrel filled with water that was used to test these motors. Nevertheless, one of the requirements to rent a row boat with an outboard motor was that you had to have a pair of oars with you in case the motor failed. Seeing boats with their outboard motor out of the water and being rowed back to dock was not uncommon.

In addition, virtually everyone in the marina business in Ocean City got into the sale of these outboards. Selling small pleasure boats with an outboard motor was one of the keys to success, and I saw firsthand at all three boatyards how outboard motors gradually increased in popularity.

When I was a kid, I remember seeing what we would think of today as vintage outboards, including the introduction of newer designs and higher horsepower in the 1940s to 1950s. Today, seeing a 32-foot open boat with three 250-horsepower engines is not unusual. It is a far cry from how it was not too many years ago, when a little row boat with a five-horsepower outboard would be sputtering down the water.

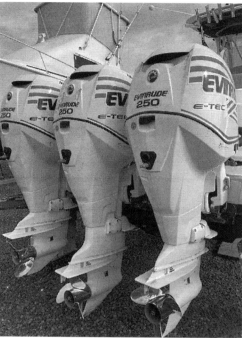

Outboard motors, then and now: a 1956 Johnson; and three present-day, 250-horsepower Evinrudes.

Outback Characters

Anyone who has been into boating, fishing, or any other water activity knows that you come across a variety of interesting people. Hanging around marinas or even boat shows today, you become aware that these people have much in common with you. However, as a little boy in a classic old boatyard, that experience occurs in different ways as you meet more and different people.

I just wanted to be friends with all of them, but the following three characters are the ones who were nearest and dearest to my heart.

Cooper

Of all the people I got to know behind our house, aka "outback," this one is forever ingrained in my memory. His name was Cooper, and he worked mostly at Turner's, painting bottoms and such. For many years, he was a well known figure to residents of the neighborhood, boat owners, yard operators, and workers. He knew everybody and they knew him, some for a lifetime. I have been looking desperately for a photo of him, with no luck. Maybe someday a photo of Cooper just might appear.

Cooper wasn't exactly homeless, because he lived on Sea Urchin, his old dilapidated 30-footer. In the winter months, Sea Urchin was docked next to Bart Turner's shop. In the spring, Cooper would take it over to Cowpen Island and let it float on the edge of the meadows. This was just opposite the boatyard, as Turner needed the slip to rent out for the summer. That was the only time the boat was unmoored, and it was a common sight to see Cooper in his rowboat going the hundred yards or so back and forth to Sea Urchin each day.

Cooper was a great conversationalist and would talk about pretty much everything and anything. I don't know exactly when he came to Ocean City, possibly sometime in the 1930's. I'm sure others knew more about him than I did. I do remember sitting on the stern of his boat listening to his numerous tales.

One time he let me come down below to see where he cooked his meals. It was cozy and tight but rather primitive to me. Cooper had a wood stove onboard, and in the winter time you could see and smell the smoke coming from the little chimney atop the cabin.

He was very independent and never begged for anything. I remember Mom giving me food to take to him at times. He loved her cooking and was always sincerely appreciative.

He knew every family member on the block and could tell you when we were all born. Thanks to ancestry.com, I was able to find his actual name in the 1940 Federal Census Record for Ocean City. He was 57 at the time, and the census record showed his address on our block as "boat." His real name was Roger Cooper, and he was born in South Carolina. I could not find him in any earlier federal census reports. Maybe when the 1950 census is made public, we'll know more.

Roger Cooper's name was listed on the census just below that of Cappy Wright's, which means to me that he lived at and worked for both Cappy's and Bart Turner's at different times.

One lasting virtue of Cooper's was how proper, polite, and respectful of others he was. I remember he always took his hat off when talking to my mother. He set a great example for us young kids, but we didn't realize the lessons he was giving us at the time.

This is similar to what Cooper's boat looked like. Courtesy of Steve Warnalis.

Doc Chance

Doc, another memorable character and also a friend of Pop's, was a clam digger who kept his small boat at Cappy Wright's. After returning from a day of raking in clams, Doc would load his burlap bags filled with clams onto a wheelbarrow and walk to his home in the 1200 block of Bay Avenue. I never did learn where he sold his catch or how he could ever make a living doing this hard work.

Sometimes, Mom would send me to his house to pick up a dozen clams at his back door. Doc was a quiet man and would open a few fresh clams on the dock for me to eat. It took a while for me to learn to eat and swallow a clam, but in the end I only ate raw clams for years.

Doc was one of those old baymen from days of yore with just a row boat and clam rake. Later he had one with an outboard motor.

Doc Chance on a day he went hunting with Pop and other friends.

T. Lee Adams

T. Lee Adams became Assistant Postmaster to my father in 1945, and in 1954 he became Postmaster. He was also my godfather and treated me as a son in many ways. Those that knew him, and there were many, often remember him as being "one colorful person" and a great storyteller. To say that he was in love with the bay was an understatement. He couldn't get enough of it.

Before he joined the post office, one of T Lee's jobs was that of a trolley car operator. By the time I was born, much of the system had been phased out, but I do recall some of the remaining tracks from the defunct trolleys being dug up when streets were reconstructed throughout the city. The story of this system of transportation in Ocean City is interesting and well documented at the Ocean City Historical Museum.

Around 1950, T Lee and his wife, Lil, purchased my uncle John's boathouse. The photo seen here depicts what a rundown structure the boathouse was when they became the owners. I remember helping him with the renovations, which in my case was just simple chores or cleaning up, easy stuff for an 11 year old. I was a good go-fer though. You know, "Go for this. Go for that." *"Jimmy go get me some more nails,"* or *"Go bring up some more molding from downstairs."* And yes, *"go to the store and get me a pack of Fatima's"* (cigarettes). We all become errand boys at times, especially when you are young and haven't found your gift yet.

John Svit's boathouse before it was purchased by T. Lee Adams.

To get to T Lee's property, you enter an alley off of 11th Street, between Bay Avenue and the bay. The alley ends about halfway, where you make a right turn and you're there. You still do it this way today. The house remains pretty much the same as when T Lee and his wife, Lil, lived there; however, it now has condo complexes on both sides, rather than boatyards. It still has a view of the bay, though that view has been significantly reduced, probably by half.

The boathouse was an old, two-story frame building, maybe 30 x 35 feet in size. I have no idea when it was built, but my guess is in the very early 1900s. It had an interior rickety staircase with many missing windows and doors, a real teardown at the time, but T Lee saved it. All of us had played in this run-down building for years.

T Lee fully rebuilt it with new exterior stairs that led to their second-floor living quarters and a porch with a million-dollar view overlooking the bay. The first floor included a small apartment that he rented out and a workshop where he created duck decoys made to order. Those decoys would be collector's items today.

T Lee was an avid fisherman and boatman. In 1975, Kurt Loder wrote a beautiful article about T Lee for *The Broadsider*, a weekly Ocean City publication at the time. Included in the piece was this photo of T Lee, which really depicts him to a "T." A copy of this article can be found at the museum.

Although I met many characters outback, Cooper, Doc, and T. Lee led the pack.

T. Lee Adams. Courtesy of Kurt Loder.

So What Happened?

Sometime during the 70's and 80's, all boatyard operations ceased, and the properties were sold. Buildings were razed, land cleared, and three separate condo complexes with nearly 50 units were built, plus one house on the bay. New boat slips replaced all of the old dilapidated docks.

Today, from our former back windows, you can no longer see the boatyards, boathouse, docks, bay, meadows, Somers Point, or Beesley's Point some two miles away. Instead, all you see are the backs of condominium units. UGH.

I know that my sister, Annetta, went through much pain and sorrow to see the demolition of the boatyard shops and removal of boatyard equipment, followed by the construction of new residential condos just a few feet from her backyard. However, she knew that there was little she or anyone could do to stop this modern-day process of tearing down the old and putting up the new in the name of progress and renewal. It simply happens, everywhere.

During the condo construction, Annetta would call me often and give me an update as to what was happening. I vividly remember the phone call when she said, "I can no longer see the bay." It was like she had gone blind, and it was very sad for her to lose that view she'd had her entire life.

All of these former boatyard facilities were very important for many years, both for the war effort and to the city's marine industry, long before and after the war. Once the boatyards were gone, the boat owners had to find other locations to store and service their boats. I suppose some simply gave up ownership and the lifestyle. Other towns up and down the Jersey Shore probably went through a similar phase. This leads me to ask: Where did all the boatyards go? That could be a title for another book for someone else to write.

I close this section, knowing that time marches on and that change comes, like it or not. I don't pretend to be critical of those who allowed all these changes to happen, not just on my old block, but anywhere in the city or country, for that matter. It would be a pretty dull world if it weren't for change, but there's no law or ordinance that precludes any of us to look back whenever we want to relive the past.

Looking back or reminiscing is a natural thing to do at times. I hope you do plenty of it. Let's just hope that others will someday write a similar book about the 60s, 70s, 80s, 90s, and more.

This is the view of the bay and Cappy's Boatyard that my sister, Annetta, could see from her bedroom in our childhood home, and which condo development obliterated. The house shown on the left is T. Lee Adams's, after he did his renovations. Across the bay, in the background, are meadows.

Jim Jeffries

It Runs In The Family

My sister, Annetta, was active in the Ocean City Historical Museum when it started at the old Wesley Avenue School. In fact, Annetta was a walking encyclopedia about Ocean City and its people, both past and present. Those who knew her understand what I'm saying. She would often say, "I could write a book on this town." In some ways, I think I'm writing this book for her.

I've kicked myself many times for not asking her questions or writing things down, knowing that I should have started writing when she was still alive. Annetta died in 2011, having lived almost her entire 80 years at 1116 Bay Avenue.

Here is a reprint of a nice article written by Steve Gring about my sister for the Ocean City Historical Museum newsletter, *The Binnacle*, in 2009. Thank you Steve! You nailed it.

I Remember When...

By Annetta Jeffries as told to Stephen Gring

Annetta Jeffries has lived her entire life on the island, having resided in her parents' home in the 1100 block of Bay Ave. From that vantage point, she has been able to chronicle the changing scene in this neighborhood. Her father (later the Post Master in town) and uncle built three Dutch Colonial houses in 1923 in the 1100 block of Bay Ave., and all three (Imagine!) are still standing and are occupied by full-time residents.

Annetta remembers how the Marina Mews Condo Complex has evolved over the years. Originally the location was a flower shop run by a Mr. Thorne. What an appropriate name for a floral business! The current condo residences were built in the 1970's.

At the corner of 12th St., there was a bowling alley that was a popular entertainment destination away from the boardwalk in the 1930's. Annetta worked there as a pin girl in the 1940's and also bowled at this establishment. Only within the last two years was the building- which later became a furniture store and then a tile store that was torn down to make room for new construction.

In the ten hundred block of Bay, a store that was run by the Mossbrook Family served ice cream and sold sundries. And Annetta remembers when the three story green sided building across from her home was moved to Bay Avenue from Central.

Asked about any notorious happenings along this stretch of Bay Ave., Annetta could only remember one, a murder that occurred in the 1970's. True to Annetta's vigilant style, she recalled seeing the police remove the body from the house.

One of Annetta's favorite memories is the time she spent playing in the boat house located to the rear of her property on the bay. She still has several original photos that show the structure being used to store boats on the "first floor." Annetta and her siblings, Jim and Bill would play on the second floor with discarded bowling pins from the corner alley. Those were the days when children could truly entertain themselves! Today the boat house is owned by the Bill Hughes Family and is divided into two apartments.

Boat house at 11th St Bayfront

Annetta has worked her entire life in the restaurant/food industry of the town. She spent 20 winters at the Flanders in various capacities and worked into her seventies for Hickman's Seafood which was located on Asbury Ave. In addition, she worked for 30 summers for Hogate's on the bay. She was also an active Museum volunteer when the Museum was located in the old elementary school in town.

This brief article has hardly scratched the surface of Annetta's vast memory archives. She has so much to tell about the informal, unwritten history of this barrier island that an entire series would have to be devoted to the revelations. As always, our best sources of information are the people who have lived the history of Ocean City first hand, people like Annetta Jeffries.

I Remember When:
This is a continuing feature of a series of articles designed to draw on YOUR memories of Ocean City. We welcome submissions for future newsletters to be mailed to the OCHM or e-mailed to Jean Bell jmb580@comcast.net

Ocean City Historical Museum / Spring 2009   2

My cousin Margaret and her family lived in the boathouse (as seen in the photograph embedded in this article) for a couple of summers after her husband, Ray, returned from the war. With the kind permission of the Ocean City Historical Museum.

Libraries Rock

Although our hometown libraries have a well-deserved place in our hearts, we shouldn't forget that libraries are what they are because of librarians. You know, the folks who spend their lives promoting literacy and spreading the love of books and stories to children everywhere? And by "children" I mean both those who are actually young and those who are young at heart.

I'm proud to say that my Aunt Edith Jeffries was Ocean City's very first librarian. According to the Federal Census of 1920, Aunt Edith was already working as a librarian at that time. She would have been only 20 or 21 years old. Her place of work was the city's first library, located in a little house on 9th Street, just off Asbury Avenue. Family legend has it that Aunt Edith met her future husband there, Bill Moncrief, and that it was love at first sight.

My first memory of a library was when I started 7th grade at the high school (7th and 8th grades were housed in the high school, but we weren't considered high school students until 9th grade). The public library was part of that building, on the southwest corner, with access for both students and the public. I remember there was a spiral staircase leading to books in a loft-type setup.

A couple of years later, maybe around 1952-53, the city built a separate, new and larger library on the school property. There continued to be access for both the public and the students.

Then, about 20 years ago—I'm not sure about the year, this being long after I left Ocean City—the city demolished the old high school, including its library, and put up new buildings in its place. These structures consisted of a new high school, with its very own school library; and a new and much more spacious public library.

Anyhow, as I write these words, the very thought that I might actually be fortunate enough for my book to end up on a library shelf puts me on cloud 9. Never in a million years would I have thought I'd get this far. Fingers crossed that you may be reading this book courtesy of the Ocean City Public Library.

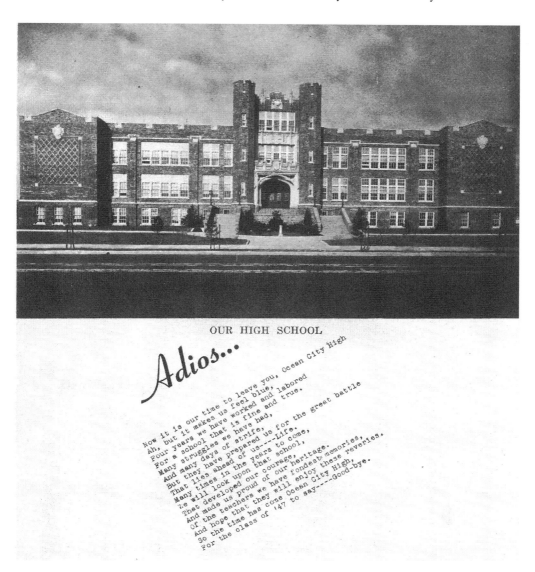

OUR HIGH SCHOOL

Adios...

Now it is our time to leave you, Ocean City High
Ah, but it makes us feel blue,
Four years we have worked and labored
For a school that is fine and true.
Many struggles of strife,
And many days we have had,
But they have prepared us for the great battle
That lies ahead of us---Life.
Many times in the years to come,
We will look upon that school,
And developed our courage,
That made us proud of our heritage.
Of the teachers we have fondest memories,
And hope that they will enjoy these reveries.
So the time has come Ocean City High,
For the class of '47 to say----Good-bye.

This 1947 yearbook image shows Ocean City High School as it was in the days when the Ocean City Public Library was in the same building.

12th Street Bowling Alley

On the corner of my block was the 12th Street Bowling Alley. This eight-lane bowling facility was another place that was a part of my youth and that of many others in the nearby neighborhoods.

My first recollection of it was that the Rone Family from Vineland owned the alleys. In 1948, it was sold to Mr. Charles Turner, father of my classmate Carol Turner Hadkte. Mr. Tatum was the manager. I remember going there with my father, and though I don't remember him actually bowling, he did keep score. We would race each other home, barely a half a block, and he'd let me win.

At some point, I became old enough to become a pin boy like my brother and his friends; there were no automatic pinsetters or anything like it in those days. You started out doing singles, which meant one alley, and as you got better you did doubles, which meant two alleys and more money. When your hands got big enough, you could hold two pins in each hand, but you started out with one pin in each.

Ducking the flying pins in the pit was a challenge. Sometimes you didn't realize the bowler had thrown the ball down the alley, and you had to move fast. Sometimes the pins won, and it hurt.

I believe we got 10 cents a game plus tip. I remember setting up pins into my high school days and coming home stinking like the city dump. It sure wasn't a healthy environment, between the cigarette and cigar smoke, no ventilation, plus the dirt of the alleys themselves, but who knew? When we weren't working, we were playing the pinball machine or outside playing kick the can, a game that required running around the building and kicking a can. I honestly don't remember the purpose of the game.

This was around the time I realized my brother, Bill, was called "Jeff" by his friends, short for our last name Jeffries. I was "Little Jeff." When Bill was out of high school, I became "Jeff." I fear to try and remember all of his friends' names, as I know I'd get it wrong. I looked up to them; after all, they were older and bigger.

I recently came across this photo of the building before it was a bowling alley. Originally, it was a service station, or filling station, as they were called back in the day. I now remember seeing the concrete repairs that were made where the pumps were removed, but I never gave that a thought at the time.

Fortunately, my friend Steve Warnalis was able to alter the exterior photo below so that it looks close to the bowling alley we all remember.

(T) This exterior shot of the bowling alley is actually a digitally altered photo of the gas station that this building used to be before it became a bowling alley. (B) The interior of the building. Both courtesy of Steve Warnalis.

The Candy Store

Continuing in the neighborhood, at the corner of 11th & Bay, was Goldy's Deli, more of a small grocery, bread, and milk store than a candy store, but oh yes, there was candy too.

The Goldy family moved there in 1949, and before that it was the Brunetti Family who owned it. I remember them very well also. It was never officially called The Candy Store, rather Brunetti's or Goldy's, but to us little boys it was where candy could be found for a nickel or so.

Although this building has also been replaced, in our hearts The Candy Store will always be there.

The storefront on the right-hand side of this familiar looking building at 11th and Bay Avenue was Brunetti's/Goldy's, aka The Candy Store.

Mr. Hess & Others

Next to Brunetti's/Goldy's store lived Mr. Walter Hess, who owned Hess Lumber Yard on the northwest corner of 11th and Simpson. The lumber yard also had two large open storage buildings a half a block away, with a railroad siding between the two. At home, Mr. Hess had a very large garage in the back, on the alley, where he would store his 28-footer.

Though he rarely used the boat, Mr. Hess rented a slip at Cappy's. In the spring, Cappy's crew would roll Mr. Hess's boat out of his garage and launch it. Of course, I was there to help with the launch.

The rest of the neighborhood consisted of Thorn's Florists, which had been vacant for some time and was torn down in the late 40s to make room for more boat storage for Turner's Boatyard. That wasn't surprising; there were about eight homes on the block, but boatyards took up a good majority of the area at that time, maybe 80%. Anyhow, the building that used to be Thorn's Florists always seemed to be a haunted house of sorts, and I was afraid to go inside it alone.

The Other Boatyard:
The Sampson Brothers

Although Moyer & Sons and Holtz Boat Works were major marine operations, the following is another Ocean City boatyard story on the bay that must be mentioned.

The Sampson Brothers were probably one of the last old-time boatyard operations in the city that I vividly remember. Born and raised in Ocean City, when they were very young boys Dick and Don Sampson trapped minnows for Frank Steelman, owner of Steelman's Party Boats at 228 Bay Avenue. As they grew older, Dick and Don did more chores for Mr. Steelman and eventually became charter fishing boat captains. In 1936, they formed Sampson Brothers at 227 Bay Ave and built small boats.

When World War II arrived, Dick served in Germany, and Don worked in Washington, building the Pentagon. After the war, the brothers resumed their business operation at 227 Bay by building boats, repairing engines, and boat maintenance and storage. In the early 50s, they purchased Steelman's and continued to grow the business. In 1989, they decided to retire and spend their winters in Florida.

The basic building shown here, which was the site of the Sampson Brothers business, has always been the same, despite having been remodeled several times over the years. Today in that building is Ocean City Boathouse Marina, owned by T.J. Heist, the son of an old friend, Tom Heist. It's good to see an enterprise like this keeping nautical life going on the bay.

Joan Sampson Weigel, Don's daughter, was a year behind me in school and a good friend. Oddly, I got to know these popular boatyard brothers not on the bay, but rather while deer hunting up in Ocean County during high school.

The Sampson Boatyard, © *Joan Sampson Wiegel.*

The Other Boardwalk

This other boardwalk, which is what people called it, extended to the bay. Starting at 30th Street and the railroad tracks (Haven Ave), it ran over a marshy area west to Bay Avenue. It continued on the other side of Bay Avenue for another 600 yards over the meadows to the bay. Quite a distance.

Picture yourself on the 30th Street side by Holy Trinity Episcopal Church, looking west. This photo, taken around 1940 of the Loder family, is what the boardwalk looked like from that vantage point. This was the pathway from the Loder home on Asbury Avenue to the end of the boardwalk, and where the duck hunting began. The structure was never in good shape and was a challenge at times to walk on, particularly with hip boots, a shotgun, and other gear.

For many years, this area never changed in appearance, until it was developed and enlarged with fill from the area where the lagoons were created. The boardwalk, bayberry bushes, and quite a bit of marshland simply disappeared.

By the way, another source says that this long-ago "other boardwalk" started at 31st Street, not 30th. Either way, it doesn't change the fact that it once existed, and still exists, in the memories of those who lived in Ocean City during its time.

The Loder family on "the other boardwalk." © *George Loder*

Jim Jeffries

The Trolley (to Atlantic City)

Whenever my mother took me to Atlantic City, where she was born, we'd go by trolley. My most vivid memory of these journeys was looking out the window while going over a bridge and seeing nothing but water. This was very scary for a little tyke like me.

With the kind permission of the Ocean City Historical Museum.

To get to Atlantic City, we took the Shore Fast Line, which started at 8th and the Boardwalk, then west through town over several bridges to Somers Point. The tracks ran parallel to the causeway, and the trolley continued north through Somers Point, Linwood, and Northfield, about a block or so west of Shore Road. At Pleasantville, it would turn east and head for Atlantic City, over the meadows and a couple more bridges. Virginia Avenue and the boardwalk was the last stop. This transportation system of orange colored trolleys ran from 1907 to 1948.

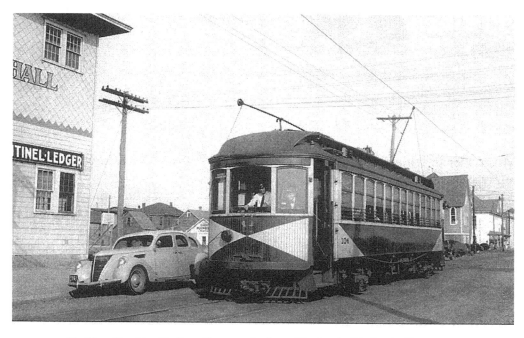

The Shore Fast Line Trolley rolling past the Ocean City Sentinel Ledger building, 1941.

When Mom and I reached Atlantic City, we would head over to Fisher's Shoe Store, and afterwards we would sometimes visit Mom's cousin who lived on Connecticut Avenue. But the shoe store was the most memorable part. They had a device you would step up onto, put your feet into an opening, and look through a viewer to see the bones of your feet to make sure the shoes fit properly. I'm sure I said "Wow."

Invented in the 1920's, this device was later discontinued when it was determined that shoe store employees had been exposed to excessive amounts of radiation over time. I guess my exposure wasn't enough to cause medical problems later in life. So far, so good.

Who remembers this gadget?

Here's one of those shoe-store foot x-ray machines, also called a fluoroscope.

Steam Locomotives

hat kid is not fascinated by a train? I mean a real big one that is so huge it scares the daylights out of you. Just imagine a train with black smoke coming out of the top and white steam coming out of the bottom—a giant that blew steam in your face, with wheels more than twice as big as you, and engineers who always waved to you. These were the trains that ran into Ocean City when we were little.

Steam locomotive at 4th street station, Ocean City, 1940s.

Today's kids don't get to see all that black smoke and white steam and hear the "chug chug" sound as the train begins to move. That sound was simply mesmerizing to me, as it was to all little boys.

The steam-generated whistles also got my attention and that of anybody else nearby. I think those whistles could be heard whether you were on the beach or in a boat on the bay. When the conductor gave the hand signal, the engineer would push a few levers, and the train would start to chug and move north or south to the next station. The stations entering Ocean City were 52nd, 34th, 24th, 14th, 10th (main), and 4th Streets; and the Gardens station.

(L) 14th Street train depot, Ocean City, 1950s. (R) Steam locomotive at Gardens train station, Ocean City, 1950.

Hissing, clanking, and other weird noises were like music with a certain rhythm that moved these mammoth machines forward and made for a memorable event every time.

Every once in a while the engine had to expel a build-up of dirty black soot, which ended up on houses and other buildings adjacent to the tracks. Think about multiplying that by thousands of coal-fired locomotives around the country. By today's standards, this would be considered an environmental crisis but probably wasn't given a thought back then.

When nobody was looking, my friends and I would put a penny on the track and watch it get flattened. Kids all over the country would do that over the years and probably still do to this day—and it's no doubt a federal crime. You did that too, right?

The first steam engine to Ocean City was in 1884, and no one ever thought this era would come to an end, at least not me. Nevertheless, steam locomotives were phased out around the country, and within only a few years, diesel-fueled engines replaced them. 1957 marked the last of the steam locomotive in Ocean City.

These beautiful trains certainly played a crucial part in our country's development, and though my hometown's section of the nationwide rail system was just a drop in the bucket, for more than 70 years those six or seven miles played a very important role in Ocean City's early growth.

For me, taking one of those steam locomotives to Philadelphia back then was like how a kid today would feel going on his first ride in a jet plane. I was seven years old or so and remember being very excited and couldn't take in all the sights fast enough, especially when we were going over the scary Crook Horn Bridge, the one leaving the island toward Palermo. I also remember that the drinking water on the train tasted awful; Mom said it was "Camden water." Still, we had no idea back then just how excellent our own water in Ocean City was. Ever think about how good our water tasted?

Another steam locomotive.

Although most little boys like me were in awe of these giant locomotives, in my case I wonder if it may have been something in my genes. My maternal great-grandfather Thomas Reeves Clayton was the engineer who drove the first train into Atlantic City and the first into Cape May too. His son, my grandfather Frank T. Clayton, was also a celebrated engineer for the Pennsylvania Railroad and did mostly Washington, New York, and Philadelphia runs as well as some South Jersey runs, accumulating one and a half million miles in his career. Both of these men were gone before I was born.

(L) 24th Street Station. (R) 34th Street Station.

Oddly enough, I didn't know much about my railroad ancestors until I started to create my mother's family tree on ancestry.com. This is when I also discovered that a number of mother's half brothers from the Pleasantville area were railroad men as well. I have obituary clippings, photos, and other family mementoes where I learned these facts. I wish I had been more inquisitive about my family's past when more of my relatives were still living. When I was a boy, Mom just told me my grandfather "worked on the railroad" and never mentioned that my great-grand-father did so as well. For all I knew back then, they could have been conductors or part of the gang that laid track.

Many books have been written about trains to the Jersey Shore, all worth reading.

51th St. Station.

10th Street Railroad Station (And More Train Stuff)

Built in 1891, the 10th Street Station is now on the National Registry of Historic Places. I don't think it changed a bit over the years, though the original building had some sort of cupola on the roof. Probably the same architect back in the day designed all the train stations in the state, maybe the country, because they're all pretty much the same. The station also seemed to be dirty all the time, thanks to the coal-fired steam engines depositing soot on the building over the years. Never once do I remembered the station being power washed or even hosed down. You felt dirty just looking at it, particularly the windows.

I can still picture taxi cabs backed up to the curb with their trunks open, waiting for newly arrived passengers to accept the waving hand of a cabbie such as my friend John DelCorio's dad, who was a part-time Yellow Cab driver. In a matter of

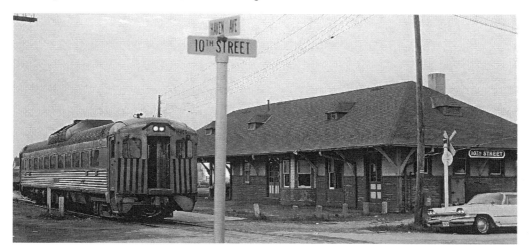

Budd car at 10th Street station. Courtesy of Steve Warnalis.

minutes, maybe six to ten cabs would have their fares and be on their way to a hotel, rooming house, or private residence.

While train passengers were disembarking, parcel post, mail, and other freight was off-loaded onto big push wagons and rolled a few feet to the freight building or to a mail truck. Meanwhile, my cousin and I, or whoever I was with, would try and talk to the engineer, yelling up at them stupid questions about the train. If only I had known back then that not too many years before, my grandfather and great-grandfather would have been sitting up in a similar locomotive cab as engineers somewhere in South Jersey or beyond.

No matter where you live in Ocean City, you don't have to walk far to get to the railroad tracks. My friends and I would take the shortcut to school by walking through the 10th Street Station property. That shortcut worked for both Central Avenue School and OCHS. Located on the north part of that block was a small path through some knee-high weeds that bordered West Avenue, pretty much where McDonald's parking area is located today. This path got rather muddy when it was raining.

My other memories of the train station are when my mother's Aunt Hattie would come to visit us from Philadelphia. My job was to meet her at the train station and carry her suitcase home. After the first time, I brought my wagon with me, as her suitcase, though small, was heavier than I was.

Now you might ask, how did they change the direction of the train?

I clearly remember my brother walking me up the tracks to about Third Street and watching how the trainmen changed the direction of the steam engine and coal car. I would have never believed how they did that without watching it happen in real time. The word "cool," as we know it today, wasn't invented yet, but that's what it was to me.

The railroad method of turning trains to go in the opposite direction was done by using something called a wye, pronounced "why." A wye was a Y-shaped joining of tracks that was specially laid out to turn trains around. There were many variations of this system, but here's how they did it in Ocean City.

Trains heading north into the city eventually came to a dead end and had to go south to leave the island. Trainmen would uncouple the passenger cars from the engine and coal car on a siding, and then only the engine and coal car proceeded north for a very short distance on a curve.

A switch was thrown, and the engine would back up on another curve until it was headed in a more southerly direction. From there, it moved past the siding where the passenger cars were sitting, stopped, another switch was thrown, and the engine backed up and reconnected to the cars. Bingo! The train changed directions. The passenger cars didn't care which way they were headed, as the conductor would simply change the direction of the backs of the seats.

Until 1957, if you lived in the general area of 2nd and 3rd Streets and Haven Avenue and towards Bay Avenue, chances are your home was right around the spot where the trains changed direction. Please see the map on these pages. At some point, the tracks were eventually removed from this area.

After my brother took me to watch the trains change direction, I couldn't wait to go home and lay down my Lionel train tracks on the attic floor and do the same thing. And it worked! I was pretty proud of myself when I did that.

I also remember the watchman's shack at 9th Street. The watchman had a simple job, which was stopping traffic by using a sign on a pole, and then letting the train pass. There was a little shack, about 6 x 6, for him to sit in between trains on the northeast corner of the crossing. I do remember stopping to talk to the watchman at 9th Street. I think he was happy to talk to anyone, just to relieve his boredom.

The speed of the train was pretty slow through town until it got past 52th Street, which was the last stop before it went over the Crook Horn Bridge toward Palermo. I don't believe other streets had crossing gates, just flashing warning lights.

Lumber, Coal, and Freight

Every chance we got, we would watch the freight trains maneuver in and out of the various sidings to uncouple different cars with the product they were carrying. There was coal for the gas company co-generation plant on 11th Street and also for a private coal yard across the street. There was also lumber for the four lumberyards: Berger Lumber, Hess Lumber, Shoemaker Lumber, and Powell-Van Gilder Lumber. Each had its own siding for delivery.

Having this experience as a kid at the end of the steam locomotive era is so memorable. At the time, freight trains seemed to come to town about once a week or so, and I never realized their days were numbered.

A few last words about trains:

After graduating high school, I went to the Peirce School of Business Administration in Philadelphia and commuted every day from Ocean City. This was shortly after the transition from coal-powered locomotives to Budd Rail Diesel Cars, which means I'd missed the chance to take steam locomotives to school by just a short time. My trips to school in the Budd cars were not very memorable, but I did meet several daily commuters who had made this trip for 20, 25, even 30 years. Maybe they were happy to get rid of the old way, with all the smoke and steam. Who knows?

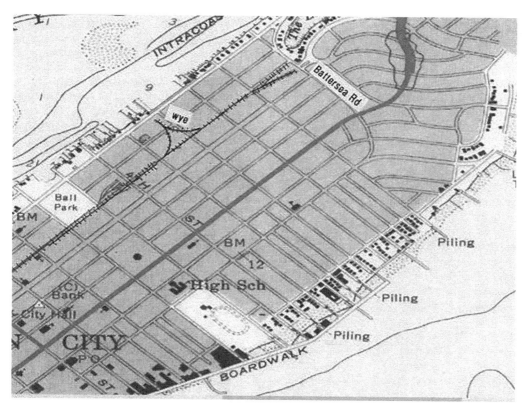

This is a map of the wye, the best place to be if you wanted to see the trains change direction. With the kind permission of the Ocean City Historical Museum.

Bicycles and Other Means

One of the first things everyone learns to ride is a tricycle, which is easy to do. After Mom sets some early boundaries, she lets you ride the entire block. That's a big step, but then came the two-wheeler, with my brother teaching me how to ride it. That's what big brothers are supposed to do.

Like many of you, I had my share of hand-me-down clothes and toys throughout my childhood, including my brother Bill's small two-wheel bike. One year my brother and I got brand-new Shelby bicycles for Christmas. I rode that bike until I got my driver's license.

Before bicycles, my cousin Donald and I had home-built scooters. We even rode them once in the Halloween Parade. Not sure what the point of that was, and can't recall how we were dressed up, but we had numbers pinned on us as entrants.

To build these scooters, we would get orange crates from DeHart's grocery store on the corner. Uncle John would cut a four-foot-long 2 x 4 board and nail an orange crate to one end of it. On the bottom of the board, he would screw half a roller skate to the front end and the other half of the skate to the back end. Top it off with a wooden handle, and you have a homemade scooter.

Uncle John made us construct the next set of scooters so that we would learn how to do it. Riding something you made yourself was a big deal. They were also very noisy. Imagine the sound of metal roller skates on concrete for hours on end.

Orange-Crate Scooter

Our scooters looked a lot like the one in this picture (Popular Science, July 1939).

Music

We always had a piano in the house. My sister played some, but my brother somehow got out of taking lessons; not me, however. At the age of five, I started taking lessons at Mrs. Sharp's house, which was on Wesley Avenue near 5th Street. My friend Tommy Adams also took lessons from her, but unlike me, he learned fast and could play pretty well.

A few years later, Mr. Oldfield from Northfield came to the house to give me lessons, and Mom made me practice, practice, practice. I hated it; however, I survived eight years of that torture.

I never could play without reading sheet music. To this day, it drives me nuts to watch people who can sit down and play the piano with no sheet music and nothing but a smug smile on their face. Honestly, it is just pure envy on my part.

I hate those guys.

Although I stopped the piano lessons at the end of the 8th grade, it wasn't the end of my musical career. I was in the high school band from the 7th grade: trumpet first, then the baritone horn. Although football in my freshman year put an end to the marching band for me, I did continue playing in the band even into my senior year and enjoyed it. Walking up the spiral staircase to Mr. Wiel's band room in the tower of the old high school brings back those band memories, as it does for many other former high school band members. Maybe you were one of them.

Church

When your mother is one of the pillars of the church, you go to church, like it or not.

Holy Trinity Episcopal Church at 11th and Central was where we attended. Pop didn't go, but Mom would drag him to work at church suppers because he had a background as a butcher. She always had me washing dishes and other chores.

Mom's church involvement didn't end with suppers: She also made all the vestments for the priests, including the embroidery detail, and she was in the church choir for years. The choir would often practice at our house, which is when I always found something else to do; it was just too much noise for this little guy. Little did I know that in a few years I would discover that Mom's friend Mr. Ralph Jarvis, who was one of the choir members, was also the famous (in our town) Mr. Jarvis, the high school English teacher.

Holy Trinity Episcopal Church. Courtesy of Steve Warnalis.

Church was where I got to know a lot more adults and kids from other parts of town, like Father Richard Bailey. My friends and I all thought Father Bailey was super, because he had a big model train platform on the third floor of the parish house next door to the church. It was the biggest train layout I had ever seen, and he would let us take turns running the trains.

Following him was Father Vaughn. He had two sons a little younger than me, and one was the smartest kid I ever knew. My friends and I would ask him what we thought were hard questions, and he always knew the answers; he probably was a genius.

Father Vaughn liked to wrestle. He would clear an open space on the floor in the rectory, teach us different holds and other moves, and take on three of us at a time. Years later, in 1959, he would preside over my wedding ceremony at the church.

For most boys, becoming an acolyte or altar boy was part of the natural progression of things, especially when you had no choice. Although I have no regrets, I sure did fight it at the time. Mom also expected me to join the choir when I was old enough, even though my brother and sister never had to. Sometimes the baby of the family gets a raw deal.

My friends Frank and George Wickes also sang in the choir, as their mother was the choir director and organist. George sang a solo at our wedding. Eventually, George went to California for nine years. On his way back, he stopped in Columbus, Ohio to visit Vince Evangelista, my classmate who was living and working there at the time. George never left Columbus and has been there for the last 51 years. What was he thinking? As for Vince, Florida was his final destination, where he enjoyed a very long musical career.

In Memoriam: Frank Wickes

Frank Wickes sadly passed away shortly before the publication of this book. Frank played clarinet in the school band and had a natural musical talent that he turned into a great career, spending 51 years as a band director in two high schools and two universities. For the last 30 years of that career, he was the band director of The Golden Band from Tigerland at Louisiana State University (LSU) and received numerous national awards. If you Google "Frank Wickes LSU," you will be amazed.

In addition to his musical talents, Frank Wickes was an outstanding athlete as well as a good student. He had a fastball that smoked, was a high jumper on the track team, and was captain of our high school basketball team when we won the Group 1 New Jersey State Basketball Championship in 1955.

Frank's proud father was a high school custodian. I often think that Frank's great musical career started at our church, 11th & Central.

My friend Frank Wickes. May his memory live on. Courtesy of Ed Goldberg.

The Big Parade

Ocean City always had a Halloween Parade down Asbury Avenue from 6th Street to 12th Street. It was a big deal then, as it is today, and has been a great tradition for our small town for about 66 years. For years, the most popular band in that parade was the Pitman Hobo Band. Can you imagine getting away with a politically incorrect name like that today?

This small group of about 20 men were, in fact, dressed up as "hobos." They weren't a slick marching band, but they sure could play. In addition to very casually walking the parade route, the group would sit down on the street in front of City Hall and perform the greatest music you ever heard. That is my memory anyway.

I've often wondered if that band is still around today, and to my surprise they are and never changed their name. Formed in 1946 in Pitman, New Jersey, the Pitman Hobo Band's appearances in Ocean City coincided perfectly with my childhood. You must go to their site: www.originalhoboband.org. Photos tell the story. As for me, I'm happy to have learned of their continued existence.

Garbage, Trash, And The Dump

Why the subject of garbage is important here and part of this book is beyond me, but it's just one of those stupid memories. Unlike today, there were no garbage disposals or plastic bags back then. It was just real-life garbage, god-awful stinky, smelly food scraps that you put into a separate, small garbage can outside the back fence.

The city picked up regular trash in an open truck, but we also had what we called an "open garbage only truck." If I recall, the garbage truck was owned by a pig farmer from off-shore (all of us from the Ocean City area know that "offshore" means Marmora, Palermo, Petersburg, and Tuckahoe areas). This man would pick up all the garbage in town and then feed it to his pigs. My memory of the awful smell that came with those open trucks is a visceral one; this was a stench that seemed to sink into your belly and lingered for some time after the truck left the alley. In the summer, the smell was ten times worse. I bet some of you old folks recall a similar experience.

When Mom said, "Take out the garbage," you knew what you had to do, like it or not. This very primitive system went on for many years. I don't think they feed garbage to pigs anymore. Thank the Lord!

Enough of this subject! I hope you can visualize the scene and appreciate the special olfactory effects I have provided.

Okay, I lied. I have a bit more to say about trash. When I worked for Mr. Harp at Hogate's Restaurant, I would ride with him in his truck to unload the restaurant trash and garbage each night at the city dump. Some may be surprised to learn that the city dump at that time was at 28th Street, off Bay Ave, in front of the idle incinerator. The dump often caught fire, which of course added more smell. When the fire engines passed our house, chances were that the dump was burning.

The Famous Incinerator

One of the landmarks, if you want to call it that, was the incinerator at 28th Street off Bay Ave. This facility was built around 1930. Believe it or not, there were two earlier proposals to build an incinerator. One location was off the causeway between Ocean City and Somers Point. The other was at 6th and West Avenue. Egad, what were they thinking? Fortunately they settled at 28th Street on the meadows side.

For some reason, this incinerator was used very little and remained idle for many years, and this "landmark" was finally demolished in 1965.

The famous incinerator. With the kind permission of the Ocean City Historical Museum.

Pop and His Friends

P op didn't do much fishing, but he and his friends sure liked to go offshore hunting for just about everything. Pop and his pals had a hunting club called Cooper Swamp Gun Club, and he would take me there when they got the place ready for deer season. Outfitted with a kitchen, dining room, and a room with about 20 bunk beds, the building was hardly a rustic lodge for the rich and famous, but they all enjoyed the camaraderie with one another.

Pop was the head cook of the gun club and, being a butcher by trade, he was also the one who dressed the deer they shot. Pop and his gun club group also went hunting for "snappers"—not fish, but turtles—and I went along with them on several occasions. They would simply go into a swampy area and poke around with poles that had a long steel end. When they hit something hard, it was probably a snapping turtle. One of the men would reach down, grab the creature, and put it into a burlap bag, without getting bitten. I wanted no part of that daring and challenging process.

Before giving Mom the turtle meat to make snapper soup, my father would remove the little turtle eggs and bury them in our backyard.

Some weeks later, the eggs hatched from the ground. We would find these little baby turtles all over the place, occasionally on the other side of Bay Ave. I would help Pop and his friends catch as many baby turtles as we could, put them in a burlap bag, and set them free in an appropriate area offshore. Recycling at its best, or is it restocking?

As for Mom's snapper soup, it was one of her specialties, and Pop's gang of about 10 would come to the house for this feast. You'll never see a happier group of men than they were. It was like Thanksgiving for Men Only. Rabbit and deer meat, clams, and oysters were also served. They loved Florence and her cooking,

As for me, my stomach didn't like the food or where it came from. But of course I still had to help do the dishes.

Every once in a while, Pop and his gun club friends would stop at Coney's Bar, just over the 34th Street Bridge. I'd sit with them and have a Coke, not having a clue as to what they were drinking. For many years, Coney's was the only structure on that stretch of road. Today on that site stands Yesterday's Restaurant Tavern, which was converted from Coney's original building. For some it was like going to Somers Point for a drink, but closer.

It seemed to me that Pop always made a point to include me whenever he was doing the outdoor thing with his friends. Looking back, I must say it was one of my building blocks. I learned what real friendship was all about by watching their interactions. Some readers may recognize the names of two of these friends: George Meyers, high school principal, and Clare Faust, owner of a men's store.

Pop and his friends (Pop's the one with the apron) at the Cooper Swamp Gun Club.

The Family Car

Talk about a vague memory: Pop owned a black, four-door 1932 DeSoto. My clearest memory of this car is when it was sitting on blocks in our one-car, dirt-floor garage, which had no doors or windows. I also remember that my cousin Donald and I played in this car as little kids. I don't know when it was purchased or when it was actually removed from the garage, but I do have the 1943 New Jersey registration. A few family photographs show the car in the background.

I have a few memories of riding in this car, but my guess is that it was taken out of use after having been damaged or flooded in the 1944 hurricane and never repaired and never replaced.

After that, I guess we got along pretty well without a car. Mom never drove, and Pop often walked to the office. Sometimes he came home by taxi or was dropped off by a friend. As for food shopping, I have no recollection of loading groceries into the back of any car. I do, however, remember helping my mother carry groceries home from the Acme Market, which was then in the 800 block of Asbury Avenue and was also where my Aunt Mary Jeffries worked as a cashier for many years. Of course my brother and sister had to carry bags home too; somehow we simply managed the food shopping routine on foot.

A Pause Here

I can't help but wonder if anyone reading these accounts has any flashbacks of their own childhood and things you had to do to help around the house. No matter where you're from or when you grew up, I imagine you must have similar recollections of events and people that I do. I hope your memories are good ones too. I'm keeping my promise by bouncing around a bit. Now back to business.

The Appointment

From the founding of our country until 1971, local postmasters were political appointments made by the President of the United States. No, my father didn't know FDR, but he did know a Mr. French Loveland, a lawyer and head of the local Democratic club or party. I think that many in the country were Roosevelt Democrats at the time, including my father.

As I understand it, one day in 1935 Mr. Loveland suggested that my father apply for the position of Ocean City Postmaster. At the time, Pop owned a grocery/meat market at 860 Asbury Avenue and somehow had managed to survive The Great Depression.

After he completed the application process, Pop was appointed Ocean City, New Jersey Postmaster in June of 1935 at a salary of $3,300 per year. After 1971, postmasters had to apply through the U.S. Federal Civil Service system for this position. That change put an end to politically connected appointments.

Fortunately, I have copies of my father's application process and letters from US Postmaster General James A. Farley, a Roosevelt protégé and political advisor. I also have the large framed appointment document signed by President Roosevelt and James Farley.

When I was born three years later, I was named James after James Farley, and my middle name is Franklin after you know who. Not a bad start for a kid.

If none of this had ever happened, my name could be different and/or I could be cutting meat opposite City Hall today, but I doubt it. I think they call it destiny, fate, or dumb luck.

The Office

When my dad began as postmaster, the post office was located on 8th Street between Asbury and Central Avenues. In 1937, a new post office was built at 9th and Ocean Avenue and remains at that location to this day. I recall Mom saying, "Your father's at the office," and when I was very young, I never knew what that meant nor cared much, as I was too busy playing and doing other things. Actually, I don't think most young kids think about where their dads worked or what they actually did, though there comes a time when you begin to learn and understand what all of that means. For example, I knew that my Uncle John was a carpenter, because he had a truck and a big shop next door with lots of tools.

One day, when I was around seven years old, Pop took me to The Office, which was, in fact, The United States Post Office at 9th and Ocean Avenue, where he was The Postmaster. What was surprising was how many people worked at the post office and that he was the boss. That was a big revelation, but it took some time for me to get the picture.

Anyhow, Pop showed me his big office facing the corner of 9th and Ocean, which had a big walk-in safe and his name on the office door facing the lobby. He also told me that our mailman who delivered mail to the house was his cousin Eddie Jeffries. Eddie would read everyone's postcards and knew everyone's business. This was an open and laughable secret.

When I was nine or ten years old, Pop gave me a summer job at the post office. It was certainly not an official one, but to me it was a job. He more or less let me do whatever I wanted inside this big building. I virtually had the run of the place: I got to know all the clerks, mailmen, parcel post drivers, and janitors. I even had my own time card that I punched in and out. Eventually I had my own set of keys on a chain that opened mailboxes throughout town. Hard to believe, but true.

I didn't get in anybody's way, but ended up helping all of them do their respective jobs and carried myself as one of them. I would even go with Mr. Bert Costigan and his wife, who had a contract to deliver mail to Beesley's Point, Marmora, and Palermo. Mr. Costigan would drive, and his wife would put the mail in the roadside boxes, a little different process than in the city. I would have lunch at their house in Marmora.

At times I would ride on the parcel post truck and help deliver packages to boardwalk stores. Later each day, we would back up to Shriver's Saltwater Taffy and load hundreds of boxes of taffy to be mailed throughout the country. We also went over to the Ocean City Sentinel-Ledger building to pick up the weekly issues that were to be mailed to each residence.

Back then, the workers received their pay in cash envelopes every two weeks. Pop would always have an envelope for me, which was about $15, obviously out of his own pocket.

If Pop were the postmaster today, with his 10-year-old kid running around the place and riding on parcel post trucks, he would probably be in big trouble. I don't know how he got away with this; maybe it was just the times we were living in then.

Today, the newspaper headline would read:

**Postmaster Jeffries jailed
for letting 10-year-old son work at post office**

Although I got to know many, if not all, of the employees at the post office at that time, I want to tell you about two special people that I got to know very well.

George Dukes and His Old Truck

Only a few living today would recognize this name, but George Dukes is another character from my young days at the post office. To me, George was very old, around 75 at the time. He was a small man and always had a little cigar dangling out of the side of his mouth. His grandson John Carew, the late Ocean City optometrist, was a childhood friend and classmate of mine.

George Dukes drove a 1928 Ford Model T box truck, which always caught the eye of many people as it passed through town. He also had a contract with the post office to pick up and deliver mailbags to and from the 10th Street railroad station and the post office. When the train pulled in, George would load the outgoing mailbags onto the baggage car, then unload the incoming mailbags into his relic of a truck, and I would always help him load and unload the mailbags at the post office and train station. In those days, there may have been as many as four or so trains a day in the summer.

George would let me ride in the back of the truck, perched on top of the mailbags, or up front with him. Either way, it was a thrill.

Without question, George had the oldest truck in town; at times it had to be cranked up to get it started, though now that I think about it, the truck was only 20 years old or so at the time.

When George died in 1959, he was about 87 years old and was truly a memorable character in my life. There were numerous other postal workers I got to know, and I learned a little bit of everything from all of them.

Next is another person whose friendship extended far beyond the post office.

George Dukes's famous 1928 Ford Model T box truck. With kind permission of the Ocean City Historical Museum.

Dick Grimes

I can't leave this subject of the post office without writing about Dick Grimes. It was around 1946 or so when I first got to know Dick, and I was about nine years old. He was a couple of years out of the service and was working at the post office as an inside clerk. He took a liking to me, as he did with just about everybody. Dick was always in motion, always doing something like sorting mail or other chores. I would stand next to him in awe, watching him sort letters into little pigeonholes with machine-gun rapidity. There seemed to be a rhythm to what he was doing. The "click, click" sound of letters hitting the wooden slots was an incredible and melodic sound.

I remember asking him, "How can you do that so fast"?

"Jimmy," he said, "if you did this all day, you would be fast too."

That answer has never left me to this day and was but one of the many lessons I learned from the famous Dick Grimes.

Dick Grimes. Courtesy of the Grimes family.

A few years later, when I was around 12 or so, some of us were playing baseball on the field opposite Dick's house on 6th Street. Dick would often come over and show us the basics and teach us other fundamentals of the game. He thoroughly enjoyed being our mentor and unofficial coach.

Quite frankly, I wasn't very good at baseball, but I wanted to be with my friends. One day, Dick put his arm around my shoulder and asked, "Have you ever thought about going out for the track team when you get to high school?" I didn't realize it at the time, but he was telling me I didn't have much of a future in baseball and I should try another sport when it came time.

A few years later, I became a miler on the high school track team. I guess I unknowingly remembered Dick's message. He was like a father to so many kids for such a long time and a great friend to many.

Dick was a good friend of my brother, Bill, and they would go hunting and skiing together. One day, decades after I first met Dick, I was skiing up in North Jersey with my daughter, Brenda, who was about eight at the time, and we met Dick and Bill on the slopes. Dick was happy and excited to teach Brenda how to ski. He hadn't seen her since she was an infant, a day in which he held her like a grandfather.

After giving Brenda some skiing instruction, he told her, "Now Brenda, go up the little hill and ski down to me and do what I taught you."

My little girl asked, "How will I find you?"

"I'm the only one here with a yellow jacket," Dick said. "Just look for me."

As Brenda headed for the ski lift, Dick and I had quite a laugh, both knowing that he was probably the only Black man on the mountain. Dick and I revisited that story about a year before he died, at Wesley Manor where he had been living. He laughed like it was yesterday.

This is one of my favorite memories of a great guy. So many others from Ocean City have similar recollections of this legend.

In 2014, Dick passed at the age of 96. I felt I had the strong responsibility to represent my deceased family members at his funeral service, which was held at the Ocean City Tabernacle.

Do you have a Dick Grimes story? I bet you do.

Jobs, Jobs, Jobs

Like all kids, I did pretty much everything one could do to make money in Ocean City, except being a lifeguard. We all did something, and many did a lot of everything. Places to work were plentiful for teenagers in the summer; it was just the nature of a seashore town. There was no excuse for not working, and I'm sure that hasn't changed much over the years.

In addition to trapping minnows that we sold to May's Boatyard and Basin, I cut neighbors' lawns with their mowers (we didn't own one). I also hung awnings for Mr. Mille across the street, then for Ken Baker, both of whom were in the awning business. Unfortunately, I didn't realize I had a problem with heights until one day I panicked up on a long ladder while putting up a third-floor dormer window awning. Mr. Baker had to come get me down. That was a know-your-limits wake-up call for sure.

One of my more earthbound jobs was delivering *The Philadelphia Bulletin* on Asbury Avenue and West Avenue, between 6th Street and 12th Street. Mrs. Graham ran the paper delivery operation from a store between 8th and 9th Streets on Asbury Avenue, exactly the property that Mr. Stainton later added onto his store.

This was another of my first real lessons in the free enterprise system. I collected from our customers once a week, and Mrs. Graham would figure out how many papers we delivered, which were "our costs." We got whatever was left over. We also had to buy an extra large basket for our bicycles so that we could carry the papers.

I was shocked at how meager my first "profit" was. As a result, I learned how to get more customers and made sure they paid up. I think that's what you're supposed to do, right?

I also sold papers on the beach, but it was hard work trudging through the sand with a heavy bag full of newspapers at that young age.

That job didn't last long for me, but some of my friends did very well.

Years later, many of us treasured the experience of having been a newspaper boy. In any case, it was a valuable work experience that molded our lives.

Long gone are the newspaper boys. Too bad.

It's not WHAT you know, but WHO you know.

Outback one day, Mayor Bowker, who kept his boat at T. Lee Adams's house (which was behind our house), asked me if I wanted a summer job and did I have "working papers." I had no idea what that meant, but he said he would take care of it. As a result, my first job with the city was working at the tennis courts at 6th Street, where the "new" high school now stands.

Over the following two years, my high school friend and classmate John Del-Corio and I worked in the public works department cutting grass, planting flowers, setting up bleachers for the baby parade, and anything else they wanted or made us do. It was good work for two football players, and we would drink a quart of chocolate milk for lunch just to put on weight.

Being a little naïve, I didn't realize at the time that I had a bit of an advantage because I knew the mayor. I never applied for those summer jobs; I just got them. But Mayor Bowker wasn't my only connection.

Because my sister worked for years at Hogate's Restaurant, which was at the foot of the 9th Street Bridge, I got a job there as a dishwasher. When I was a bit older, I worked at Harry's Inn as well as Mac's Restaurant in Somers Point, because my brother worked at both places. Before I married, I also worked as a furniture salesman at Stainton's Department Store. Mr. Stainton had someone call me to come in. Then of course there was my job at the post office.

I should have kept a diary of my work experience, as I just can't recall when and where every job was, and I'm sure I've forgotten some. I just remember always working, as many kids still do to this day, in Ocean City, known to many as…

America's Greatest Family Resort

I don't think any of us in Ocean City had a clue as to the importance of our city's resort business until we got to high school. All we knew was that a lot of people came in the summer and were gone by Labor Day. One of the strangest recollections I have of the resort season is from when I was little. Cousin Donald and I would go to the corner of 9th and Bay Avenue and count all the cars with Pennsylvania license plates. What the purpose of that was, I have no idea, just something for two young boys to do, I guess. But later we realized that those Pennsylvania license plates were a sign that there was money to be made by the young people of Ocean City—if they wanted to work, which many of us did.

Speaking of 9th and Bay Avenue, back then there was a gas station on every corner of that intersection: Esso, Amoco, Atlantic Richfield, and Gulf, where we went to get free air for our bicycle tires. Texaco was up on the corner of 9th and West Avenue. Now that I think of it, I never worked at a gas station, pumping gas.

Today it's hard to find a gas station in Ocean City, let alone one where a kid could get a summer job or after-school job, and certainly not at 9th and Bay. To my great surprise, I understand that now there is only one gas station in town, which is way down on 34th Street. What's America coming to? I've given up trying to count how many gas stations existed in Ocean City, say around 1950. You try it.

But I digress. When we were young kids, there were so many life lessons about working that none of us would trade for a nickel. I hope these stories about my jobs as a kid will take you back to your own young days of working and how you got those various jobs. Try and make a list; it may make you smile.

Boardwalk and The Beach

When I was real little, the only time I went to the beach was when my Uncle Paul and Aunt Marion would come up for a few days from Washington, D.C. This was probably because Pop never went to the beach and never learned to swim. When I was a bigger kid, I went to the beach more often. Although I was pretty much a bay rat, I also got my share of seaside fun, building sand castles and going in the water, just like kids today.

One time, I got caught in an undertow till a lifeguard, who happened to be standing knee-deep in the water close by, grabbed me. That experience shook me up, but I learned about the red flag and what it meant; it was probably the most important lesson in my life.

One of my first money-making enterprises was collecting empty soda bottles on the beach. My cousin and I would ask beachgoers if we could have their empty soda bottles. We would then return them to a little hot dog stand on the beach, next to The Flanders' hotel pool. We were paid two cents per bottle. I guess we were independent contractors and didn't know it.

In high school, John DelCorio and I had the prime newspaper-selling location at night, which was at 9th and the Boardwalk. Saturday night was a big night, as we sold hundreds of *Philadelphia Enquirers* and *Philadelphia Bulletins*. We cleaned up. Plus it was a lot more fun selling newspapers from a single location on the Boardwalk rather than carrying them up and down the beach like I'd done a few years earlier.

As a teenager, the beach became even more important, as it did with most guys. Sitting on the beach with local girls and yes, with the ones from Philly too, was important to the progress of our maturity. How's that for a euphemism?

Downtown and Howard S. Stainton

We use the word "icon" these days to describe someone who stands far and above the rest of us. In retrospect, I must say that Howard S. Stainton fits that title. There was absolutely nothing in this man's life he didn't achieve that he sought to do. He had all the positive attributes needed to succeed, the first of which was being a man of God, and everything else radiated out from there.

Bustling downtown Ocean City, circa 1953. Stainton's department store can be seen in the background. Courtesy of Steve Warnalis.

It's pretty much a sure bet that if you're from Ocean City, the first thing you think about when "Downtown" comes to mind—for us that was from 6th Street to 12th Street on Asbury Avenue and spilling off to the sides—is Stainton's department store. Stainton's was what would be described today as an "anchor store" in a mall complex, though we had no such term back then, and no malls either.

Stainton's was where your mom dragged you from department to department and where you first sat on Santa Claus's lap. I bet your first ride on an elevator was at Stainton's too. Although I have no memory of that life event, I have no doubt it was in Stainton's department store. Do you remember the first time you rode in an elevator, and where it was?

Stainton's department store entrance, downtown Ocean City, circa 1953. Courtesy of Steve Warnalis.

I remember Mr. Stainton was always walking the floor in his store, greeting customers by name. He knew my parents well and always called me "Jimmy" as I was tagging along behind Mom. He was a master at personal relationships.

Many of us remember his original store, which was doubled in size on Asbury Avenue with an annex added over to West Avenue. I believe this massive expansion occurred sometime in the early 1950s. The vast majority of the remaining downtown merchants were also hardworking entrepreneurs, many operating family businesses for years.

Mr. Stainton's reach went far beyond his store. From his home-heating oil business to being part of an expanding building enterprise, he made his mark in all parts of town. To me, his biggest impact and legacy was his financial support of churches and charities of every kind.

Santa at Stainton's

During the Christmas season, on the third floor of Stainton's department store, Santa sat in a big chair. Kids lined up, just like they would in any other department store, waiting to tell Santa that they were good and what they wanted. At some point, we realized that Santa was a bit of a fairy tale, but we all kept quiet so that we didn't spoil it for you little ones coming behind us, a tradition that continues everywhere to this day. Oh yes, I finally realized that Santa was, in fact, Mr. Gandy, a friend of my father's. I'm sure many remember that fact.

Where is Santa these days?

1923 Christmas greetings from my father's store. Image courtesy of Steve Warnalis.

Christmas Is Coming

Every family has some sort of ritual to get ready for Christmas. For me and my brother, it was going up into the attic to bring down all the boxes that contained the Lionel trains, tracks, houses, transformer, and the rest of our model train gear. Then there was the 4' x 8' platform, out in the garage. Of course we couldn't do any of this until Mom said it was okay. We always thought that Thanksgiving Day would be a good time to set up our trains, but she never agreed to that idea. Did this happen at your house too?

Our enclosed, unheated front porch is where we laid down the platform and hooked up the track. This was an exciting time for any boy. As time went on, my brother became less interested in trains, which was fine by me; it meant I got to have them all to myself.

For years, we had the same engines, cars, switches, and other accessories. I can't remember ever buying or getting anything new. I was always envious of my cousin Donald, as he had more trains, lights, a bigger platform, and more things to hook up than I did. It just wasn't fair.

My question is: Do kids have a similar ritual with trains today as we did back then? I think not. They have all the electronic video games, computer-driven toys, and mind-numbing gadgets that have such a short life span.

SAVE THE TRAINS !!!

Car Dealerships, Circa 1950S

At a certain age, maybe around 12 or so, many young boys take an interest in cars. In the 1950s, new cars were secretly covered up until a certain date in September. All car dealers unveiled their new models within days of each other, and somehow you knew what day that would be, like September 12th, for example. It was a big deal.

Today you have no idea when the new models are introduced; plus they all look alike. Back then, we could easily tell a Ford from a Chevy or an Olds from a Cadillac. To me, the day that the new cars were presented to the public was always something to look forward to, a don't-miss event. My friends and I would ride our bikes to Palmer Chevrolet in the 1100 block of Asbury Avenue and see the "New 1953 Bel Air" or whatever the newest model was called.

These were the days when you ordered your new car and waited four to six weeks for delivery. As we all know today, we can buy a new car and drive away in it the same day we walk into a showroom.

In retrospect, I find it interesting to note how many dealerships there were in little old Ocean City. Sure, there were buyers from Somers Point, Upper Township, and Sea Isle City, but it seemed to me that there were too many dealers for the population. Let's see if we can remember them.

Palmer Chevrolet & Oldsmobile..........................1115 Asbury Avenue.

Powell Cadillac & Pontiac................................12th and Asbury Avenue.

Bishop Packard/Hudson.................................12th and Asbury Avenue.

Wallace Buick...9th Street and Simpson.

Gardens Lincoln/Mercury...............................220 Wesley Avenue.

Kaiser Frazer/Willeys..6th and Asbury Avenue.

Kurtz Ford..1st and Atlantic Avenue.

Mengel Studebaker..112 Central Avenue.

Branin & Konschak Dodge..930 Asbury Avenue.

Palmer Chevrolet also sold Frigidaire appliances, as both were GM products at the time. In addition, Palmer had a used car location at 9th and Simpson (southwest corner).

Over time, dealerships changed ownership, names, and many just went out of business. Palmer Chevrolet lasted the longest, but that franchise finally closed in 2016. Like most dealerships around the country, they moved to the huge showrooms on major highways, no longer to be found in little towns; it was simply a sign of the times.

Ocean City car dealership ads, circa 1950s. Courtesy of Steve Warnalis.

Ice Box to Refrigerator

I'm not sure when refrigerators became a hot consumer item, but in our case it was probably close to 1950. Our refrigerator was a Coldspot from Sears, and I don't believe it had a freezer at the time. For us, freezers came later.

Mom ordered all sorts of things at Sears from the catalog, even though the store itself was in the 900 block of Asbury Avenue, near Palermo's Market. You simply didn't buy things off the floor at the time. You ordered, and then your merchandise was delivered, sometimes weeks later. Receiving the big Sears catalog in the mail became an event.

This reminds me: We didn't have a clothes dryer either, even after we upgraded from a ringer washer to an automatic one. My mom and most other moms hung washed clothes on a clothesline in the backyard to dry. Often she would send me out in the dark of night to unclip the clothes and bring them inside. My stark memory of these occasions is of me, in the winter, unclipping bed sheets and towels that were so frozen they were more like sheets of plywood. I'm sure that some of you also have this type of recollection.

The Man

The Man, meaning, The Milkman, The Iceman, The Bread Man, The Egg Man, The Produce Man, The Knife Sharpening Man, The Oilman. Did I miss any? Oh yes, the Paper Boy on a bike.

The only "man" we have remaining today is the mailman and maybe the oilman. There might be a few exceptions, such as the recent resurgence of produce delivery services. Nevertheless, most of the above "men" who were part of our childhood and had been around for many years before, are gone. Not just in Ocean City, but throughout the nation. These home services, which are just memories now, were part of life in the late 40s and 50s.

Let's look back and see if you remember them the way I do.

The Milkman

In Ocean City, you were either an Abbott's Dairy or a Supplee Dairy customer. We were with Supplee, but the routine for both dairies was pretty much the same. The milkman had a little metal carrier that held maybe six or eight quarts of milk. He would place the correct number of quart bottles on your porch or wherever and retrieve the empty bottles, then go back to his specially built milk truck. Sometimes, in cold weather, the milk froze.

The Iceman

If you're around my age and lived in the era before refrigerators and freezers, you might have grown up with an icebox in the house. In Ocean City, I believe it was Shiding Ice and Stewart's Ice that delivered ice to your house. There may have been others, but we used Shiding Ice, as they were down the street from us. The Ocean City Ice Plant was at 12th Street, between the railroad tracks and West Avenue.

My friends and I would hang out near the plant's loading dock and watch workers load large blocks of ice, which had been created in the plant, from the outside platform onto the delivery trucks. Much to the disappointment of our inquisitive minds, we were never invited inside the plant to see the process of making ice.

The home delivery system was like this: You placed a card in your front window that told the driver of the ice truck how many pounds of ice you needed. I think the choices were 100, 75, 50, and 25. Mom often told me, "Stick the card in the front window." That was one of my earlier chores. The iceman would cut the desired amount from a much larger block sitting in the back of his truck. He would then put a small leather pad on his shoulder and carry the block of ice into your house.

Our icebox was in an unheated room behind the kitchen; I would guess that most houses were set up in a similar fashion. The back door was always open, and the iceman would place the ice into your icebox. He would come in unannounced, do his job, and leave.

These old iceboxes are now collectible items and used for special interior design situations. Who would have ever thought that could happen?

Let me jump to an ice-related story about a classmate of mine (class of 1956) from Sea Isle City, named Joe Romano.

Joe was a quiet, good guy, and I remembered him as working for Acme Markets in Sea Isle City. Although on occasion I would see Joe at class reunions, I never really knew exactly what he was doing since those former times, as I didn't live in the area anymore. However, I did learn at some point that Joe founded Sea Isle City Ice Company in 1965. Good for him, I thought. I had no knowledge of the fact that Joe had started this company from scratch, nor of how large the company became and still is today, with a large plant in Woodbine, 75 trucks, over 100 employees, and operating in four states. His son, Joe Jr., has been running the company since his dad passed in 2010. Retired Judge Tony Gibson can give you more on Joe Romano's success story. I love it.

Fellow classmate makes good: Joe Romano, founder of Sea Isle Ice Company. Courtesy of Ed Goldberg.

The Bread Man

Although I don't remember a bread man coming to our house, I do remember seeing the Freihofer's Bread truck in the neighborhood, so I assume others had bread delivered to their houses.

The Egg Man

In some cases, I think, the egg man was the same person as the milkman, but we had a separate egg man come to the house.

The Produce Man

Mr. Triple was our produce man and would stop at our house with his fruits and vegetables loaded in what I remember as a woody-type station wagon or small truck. Neighbors would make their way over to his vehicle to make their selections. I'm sure there were others like him, but he only operated in the summer months.

The Knife Sharpening Man

When you heard a distinctive bell sound coming down the street, you knew that it was the man who sharpened your knives. "Go flag him down," Mom would tell me, as she gathered up her knives and scissors.

In the back of his truck was a big wheel he used to do the work. That's when you saw other moms from the neighborhood standing in line holding their knives to be sharpened.

The Oilman

I know, we still have some oilmen left, but the one I remember worked for one of Howard Stainton's businesses, Seashore Oil Company. Mr. Stainton was known to let oil bills slide when times were bad and customers couldn't pay when due.

I remember Mr. Bartholomew, our oilman and a long-time Stainton / Seashore Oil Company employee who was never seen without a cigar stuck in his mouth, dragging the fuel oil hose from the truck to our tank.

Does anyone else remember Bart? His wife was Mr. Stainton's right-hand employee, and his son Bob was a friend of my brother's.

The Invention of the Century— Television

When my daughter was little, I always hesitated to explain to her, or later to my grandson, what it was like to live without a television. *He's dreaming up another story about ancient times,* was what I imagined they were thinking. I'm sure many of you have had this experience.

When I was a boy, radio was our home entertainment. This was prior to the advent of the idiot box. Looking back, it was a memorable era. Like many of you, I remember sitting at the dining room table listening to "The Shadow Knows" or "Gang Busters" or "The Lone Ranger," and a few others.

What's special about radio is that it made you visualize what was being said and where the scene was. Not so with TV. My guess is that most children born after the war did not share this radio-only experience.

In the early TV era, Boyd's TV on Asbury Ave, which was next to the Lee family's laundry, seemed to be the go-to store for a TV set and antenna. Boyd's would install the antenna on the roof of your house. There were a few others, like Scuff Electric, but I remember Boyd's.

In researching early television manufacturers, I was surprised to see so many names, most of which are no longer in business. Some of the names I remember were Motorola, DuMont, Admiral, Philco, Emerson, and RCA.

Uncle John had a TV sometime before we did, and I remember watching western movies with my cousin Donald after school. I don't think the networks had much in the way of TV programming at the time.

Another memorable part of the early TV era was "The Howdy Doody Show," which began in 1947 and ran for 12 years. It was the first children's TV show and was, without question, a national treasure. There is a lot of info online about "Howdy."

TV caught on quickly. All across the country, thousands, if not millions, of TV antennas covered the landscape. If you didn't see an antenna on a roof, you might think that was a poor family.

Well, around 1950 or so, we finally got Boyd's to erect an antenna on our roof and hook up our new Motorola TV. We were no longer poor.

A few years later, I was visiting with the Platt kids, who lived near 14th and Pleasure Avenue. It was there that I saw my first-ever, so-called color TV. The father, Mr. Dave Platt, founder of Platt's Furniture, had a black-and-white set with a separate multicolored lens that was placed in front of the TV set. It was like a large magnifying glass with colored glass and was not a very convincing color picture as we know it today. Looking back, I'm thinking, what a joke that must have been, but I guess at the time it seemed like progress.

Below is some information from the Early Television Museum (earlytelevision. org) about the companies that manufactured early color television sets. Consider the prices of these TVs in light of the typical family income at that time (around $4,200 in 1953 and 1954, according to the United States Census):

"Raytheon, Admiral, or Philharmonic may have been the first company to offer color sets for sale to the public. The first set to be manufactured in significant quantities (approximately 500) was made by Westinghouse, and sold for $1295. RCA introduced the CT-100 a few weeks later, at a price of $1000 (about 4000 were made). GE sold its 15 inch set for $1000; Sylvania's cost $1150. Emerson rented color sets for $200 for the first month and $75/month thereafter. By the summer of 1954 there was already a shakeout. A headline in the New York Times said 'Set Buying Lags - Public Seen Awaiting Larger Screens, Lower Prices.' Motorola and CBS promised a 19 inch screen at $995."

Only a handful of Ocean City families could afford them, but certainly some did initially. I honestly can't remember when we got our color TV, as my father was ill and retired on disability while I was still in high school.

This leads me back to Mr. David Platt, the man who had that crazy multicolored lens on his TV set. Mr. Platt was quite an individual and lived well into his nineties. His four sons were all near my age, and we grew up together. Their little sister Carol came sometime later.

I recall Mr. Platt coming to our house carrying a big furniture catalogue. Mom would pick out something, and he would deliver it sometime later. That is how he started his furniture business, basically door to door. In 1948, he opened his first small store on Asbury Ave. Then, in 1954, he opened a new store in Somers Point, and it remains there to this day, operated by his son David, who started working for his dad in 1958 after serving in the military.

Mr. Platt was also a Scoutmaster for the Boy Scouts and later very involved in country line dancing. I worked for Mr. Platt for a short time in his Northfield store, selling carpet. He was a genuinely nice man and a good businessman. His son Jerry, who was my close friend, was in my graduating class. In 1963, shortly after serving in the U.S. Army, Jerry was killed in an auto accident when his car went off the Somers Point Bridge. I believe he was one of the first classmates we lost.

Swimming Lessons—Really?

It is always strange for me to hear of people who were born and raised in Ocean City and yet never learned to swim. My father was one of them, but that didn't stop him or other non-swimmers from going out on a boat for fishing, clamming, or just for pleasure. Here's how I learned to swim:

My brother, Bill, would push me off Uncle John's dock and tell me to swim back to the ladder. That was it. Of course I probably struggled and was scared to death, but that was my first experience. From there, little by little, I swam a bit farther each time and finally made it to the 12th Street Pavilion. Later, and with the incoming tide, Bill and I would swim down to the 14th Street Pavilion (which no longer exists).

The big test came when you made your first swim across the bay to the sandbar on the meadow side. I might have been 11 or 12 at the time. What a stupid thing to do, and for sure Mom never knew about it, but it was a real confidence builder for a new swimmer.

Swimming at The Flanders hotel pool really didn't count. That was just playing in the water. I feel like I owe The Flanders some money, as my cousin and I would sneak in under the boardwalk through a hole in a chain link fence. I don't remember ever paying to enter, but we weren't the only ones pulling off that caper. I've heard others confess to the same high crime.

Another place to swim was at our high school. In fact, the best thing about Ocean City High School was that it had a pool. In all of South Jersey at that time, maybe only one other school had a pool.

In order to graduate from Ocean City High, you had to become a "qualified swimmer" via a swimming program that Coach Fenton Carey ran as part of phys ed.

I remember that many struggled to make that qualification, but most did it and for the better. Though to be honest, Coach Carey let some slide a bit. In fact, I can't remember anyone who failed to graduate because of this requirement.

Then there was the Junior Fair, which was a talent show of sorts that the junior class would put on in the gym and swimming pool to raise money for the class. At one of these fairs, my friend Dave Loder and I put on a skit in the pool that almost became a disaster. In the skit, we were supposed to be duck hunters, and I fell into the water from a raft, fully clothed. Dave was not in the water but noticed that I was going under and jumped in and got me to the side. It happened in seconds, and we never thought most people knew what really happened. We both should have known better and probably should have rehearsed our act. Lesson learned.

I imagine that thousands of students had fun in that old pool over the years. If it weren't for that pool, many native kids of Ocean City never would have learned to swim or become better swimmers. At the time the school was built, which was back in the 1920s, I'm sure many protested that the pool was an extreme luxury the town couldn't afford. That same mentality carries on even to this day in modern school construction.

Bill Jeffries, my big brother.

The Day the Cowboy Came to Town

Although today's kids have no idea who Roy Rogers, Gene Autry, or Hopalong Cassidy were, to my generation these movie cowboys were our boyhood heroes. When we were kids, we would do anything to go to a cowboy movie at the Village Theater and see them on the screen.

One day in 1949, we heard that Roy Rogers was going to fly into the Ocean City Airport in his own plane. Now that was a big deal. I would have been about 10 or so and rode my bike down Bay Avenue to the airport with my cousin.

I remember seeing the plane land and stop near the crowd, which included many other kids my age. The door opened, and sure enough the great Roy Rogers appeared in full regalia, cowboy hat, gun and all. Some local politicians had their picture taken with him by the plane, and within a few minutes he was gone.

I had forgotten all about this little story until recently, when I found a picture of the event for sale on eBay. The picture was of Roy Rogers and a few city dignitaries standing by the plane at the Ocean City Airport. I was in shock when I saw this photo. I hadn't even been looking for a photo or anything. I was just scanning eBay, which I rarely do.

By the time I found my wallet for my credit card, it was SOLD. I still haven't recovered from this disappointment.

The next day I asked my friend Steve Warnalis if he could find a photo of Roy Rogers. I told him it would make my day. Steve sure did come through, even though this was a slightly different shot than the one I wanted to buy on eBay.

If you Google "Roy Rogers," you'll find a thousand photos of him and his wife Dale Evans. Without a doubt, he was every boy's hero.

Roy Rogers, beloved movie hero, makes a pit stop in Ocean City. Courtesy of Steve Warnalis.

The (Future) Princess Comes to Town

Much has been written about the Kelly family from Philadelphia and their Ocean City summer home at 27th and Wesley. Frankly, none of that meant anything to me, until one day in 1954 when Grace Kelly, a new and famous movie star, visited our football practice. This was obviously a PR appearance of some kind, which was fine with me.

Sometime after that, even bigger things happened in town when the prince of Monaco, who was publicly pursuing Ms. Kelly, showed up in Ocean City to visit her family. My guess was that he was there to ask her father for her hand in marriage.

He got the green light, and Grace Kelly became Princess Grace of Monaco, and the rest, as we say, became international history, with Ocean City the benefactor.

Grace Kelly's unforgettable visit to our football practice. From left to right: Art Ford, local attorney; Wayne Hudson; Coach Dixie Howell (83); unknown; me, Jim Jeffries; Sammy Foglio (3); attorney Nate Davis; Grace Kelly; Chick McDowell; John DelCorio (low face); Joe Kennedy; Bart Stull; Dr. Charles "Binky" Hadkte (90); Will Strathman; and Coach Fenton Carey. From my OCHS yearbook, with thanks to the yearbook staff.

Pinball

From childhood and into our teenage years, pinball machines were as addictive to some of us in the 1940s and 50s as iPhones are to kids today.

According to BMI Gaming (bmigaming.com):

"Pinball machines really grew in popularity after World War II. The ten-year period of 1948-58 is referred to by some as the 'Golden Age' of pinball, due to the invention of flippers in 1947 by the D. Gottlieb Co. in a game called 'Humpty Dumpty,' and was one of the main reasons for the renewed interest in pinball machines at the time. Humpty Dumpty was the very first pinball machine with flippers!"

Back then, the pinball craze was so huge that the excitement of a NEW pinball machine at the 12th Street Bowling Alley spread like wildfire. This also occurred at other locations throughout town that had machines, and of course on the boardwalk.

What other gadget, large or small, gave rise to the modern era of hands-on electronic recreation? I submit it was none other than the pinball machine and its phenomenal popularity.

A pinball machine from this era. With kind permission of Olde Good Things,
a great place to find old good things. https://ogtstore.com/

Jukeboxes

Jukeboxes were the other mechanical devices of the day that were an important part of our lives. According to Wikipedia:

"The word 'jukebox' came into use in the United States beginning in 1940, apparently derived from the familiar usage 'juke joint,' derived from the Gullah word 'juke' or 'joog,' meaning disorderly, rowdy, or wicked."

This means that we teenagers were "disorderly, rowdy, or wicked" kids of the 40s and 50s and are probably responsible for the downfall of the teenage generations that followed. Maybe not, but we sure did idolize our Wurlitzers, with their bubbling lights and their crazy colors and designs.

These mechanical and later electronic creations are classic antiques today. They can sometimes be found in one's basement and are worth a ton of money.

What <u>Hasn't</u> Changed In Ocean City?

N o matter where we live now, we see changes happening all the time, and we get over it. Sometimes we can't remember, after a year or so, what was "there" before they built that strip mall, Wawa, or whatever. I'm sure that is true for many who return to Ocean City.

For some of us who have been away for awhile, we are of course aghast to see the changes in the town that we grew up in. I know there was cultural shock for some in Ocean City when our beloved high school was demolished and a new one erected where the tennis courts and our youth center had been located. However, I think, or at least I hope, that all of us who went through the old high school have gotten over this.

Not all of the changes are bad, obviously, though we still expect to see the same houses, neighborhoods, businesses, streets, schools, firehouses, boardwalk, rooming houses, hotels, and beach. As for me, I've come to town for short visits to see family and friends, but until recently, I never went on a self-guided tour of the city to really see the Ocean City of today. As we drive through the town, we see one example after another of change or total replacement. The post office is still in the same spot, but it looks a little different, as does The Flanders Hotel and many others. We rack our brains to visualize what sat on a particular corner where now stands a motel, bank, condo, or duplex. Many times we just can't remember. Even the bridges and causeways leading into the city are completely different.

Don't get me wrong; I understand change must and does happen, but when you have this disease called nostalgia, you feel the need to go into therapy for some reality treatment. Are you with me, or is it just me?

I sometimes have to hit myself on the head and say to myself, *hey, wait a min- ute, what do you think your parents went through from the early 1920s or so?*

Just look at the hundreds of old Ocean City postcards from bygone eras to remind yourself of what little from those early days of the city still stands today.

Those postcards and photos sure do help keep the history of the town alive in our minds, and thanks to the Ocean City Historical Museum and Facebook groups like OCNJ Chatter, we are still keeping this past alive today. This modern-day ability for so many to instantly share stories and photos both old and new on the Internet is truly amazing, and yes, very addicting to some. You know who you are.

All of this brings us back to the question: What HASN'T changed or changed very little in Ocean City over so many years? I think you'll agree with my choices, even though there are many other possibilities, but you'll have your own list, I'm sure.

Lifeguards

Fred Miller, writer, historian, and one of the foremost authorities on Ocean City, New Jersey, wrote a fascinating piece in the Ocean City *Gazette* in August 2010 on the history of the Ocean City Beach Patrol. Following are a few facts that Fred points out regarding this incredible group and its accomplishments, from its inception in 1898:

"Ocean City has been a national leader since the late 19th century when becoming only the second community in the nation, following neighboring Atlantic City to establish an official paid lifeguard service for bathers. In all those years, no one has drowned on a protected beach. Every guard takes pride in that stellar reputation. It all comes down to a well-trained lifeguard. The most important piece of equipment today is the same as in 1898—the rescue can. When the island's founders, the Lake Brothers, arrived in 1879, there were four buildings. Three of them were life saving stations. When the Sindia ran aground in December 1901, lifesaving personnel rescued 33 people."

A number of my friends from high school were lifeguards, some for many years, through college and beyond:

Ralph Platt, Jerry Platt, Gene Platt, Charlie Bowman, Tom Heist, Don Eisenhardt, Wayne Hudson, Ted Holmes, Bob Holmes, Dave Coe, Warren North, Tom Adams, Bill Cox, and Tom Oves, a friend of my brother, Bill. Charlie Bowman and Tom Oves have sons, grandsons, and great grandsons on the patrol. Sorry if I've forgotten any others.

Think of the millions of bathers who have been protected over the years by this group of unique and dedicated men and women.

There is quite a bit of written history about lifeguards, an incredible history that continues to this day. I've always connected lifeguards with the U.S. Marines. Have you heard of the slogan, "Once a Marine, always a Marine"? I think that applies to lifeguards as well. It NEVER leaves their blood. As for me, I never considered myself a strong swimmer, which is critical to being a guard. Besides, I was a bay rat.

This visual of a lifeguard stand and boat is pretty much the same as it has been for many years, and is another reason people keep coming back to Ocean City year after year. Most important is that the mission of the OCBP hasn't changed, and our visitors love their safety blanket. Cheers to the enduring Ocean City Beach Patrol.

Another day begins for Ocean City's Beach Patrol.

The Music Pier

This building remains very close to what it was when it was built in 1928. I don't believe the exterior color has ever changed either. If ever there was a clear symbol of Ocean City's Boardwalk, it is this iconic building.

I hate to admit it, but I think the last time I was inside this great hall was when I graduated with my Class of 1956. Just think, in 2028, it will be 100 years old and has hardly changed.

I wish I could remember some of the featured singers and other artists who would appear year after year, but unfortunately, I don't. Maybe you do.

14th Street Fishing Pier

Originally built in 1916, the pier at 14th Street and the Boardwalk, officially called the Ocean City Fishing Club, is the OLDEST continuous fishing club in the United States. Although severe storms damaged the pier in 1916, 1945, 1949, 1962, and 1992, hurricanes and nor'easters have failed to take away another symbol of the city's past. The pier remains a premiere historic structure of the city's beachfront.

Ironically, I have never been on that pier but appreciate its unique longevity. Maybe someday I'll get an invitation.

Another historic Ocean City pier was the 59th Street pier, which I understand was nearly as old as the 14th Street pier. The 59th Street pier was severely damaged by storms over the years until it was finally removed in 2015.

City Hall

For many years, both the police and fire departments occupied the ground floor of City Hall, with city offices and the court on the upper floors. Other than that, there is very little that has changed from City Hall's original outside appearance when it was first built in 1925. It has such a majestic look and truly represents the core of the city and its people.

Hats off to all the city officials over many years who never wavered in continuing to decorate; no, beautify, City Hall for the holidays. I'm not sure when it all started, but we all know that seeing that stately building shine year after year is a symbol of local pride.

The City's Churches

I mentioned that we would have a little history in this book. A key part of that history was the early establishment of churches in Ocean City. The Methodist minister founders of our town, three Lake Brothers and William Burrell, had a vision of creating a Christian community of churches of all denominations, some of which were founded prior to 1900 and many shortly thereafter.

Bill Pehlert, a volunteer at the Ocean City Historical Museum who has helped me in many areas of fact-finding for this book, has chronicled when these various churches became such cornerstones of the town. He writes:

"After starting the seaside resort in 1879, the Ocean City Association started summer worship services in its Tabernacle building in 1880. Soon various denominations met in existing buildings prior to obtaining their own frame churches.

"Eleven of Ocean City's current sixteen church buildings, nine of which are downtown between 7th and 13th Streets, have remained basically the same in appearance for over 100 years or close to it. Masonry buildings replaced 19th century frame buildings for First Presbyterian Church (1906), St Peter's UMC (1908), Ocean City Baptist Church (1927), and St. Augustine RC Church (1931). A frame building was moved from New York and stuccoed for St. John's Lutheran Church (1927).

"African-American church frame buildings were built or acquired—Macedonia UMC (built 1902), Tabernacle Baptist Church (acquired 1906), St. James AME Church (acquired 1907), and Shiloh Baptist Church (acquired 1912).

"Union Chapel by the Sea's frame building at the island's south end (55th St. & Asbury Ave.) has served summer visitors since 1902 and is now a year-round church. Central Ocean City Union Chapel's frame building at the island's center (32nd St. and Central Ave.) has been a summer chapel since 1916.

"Five of Ocean City's current sixteen church buildings are newer. Two masonry Roman Catholic churches were built at 2nd and 40th Streets, and recently Coastal Christian acquired Stainton's annex at 8th St. & West Ave. The Tabernacle's original frame church, built in 1880 at 5th St. and Wesley Ave., was replaced by a masonry building in 1957. Holy Trinity Episcopal Church, a frame church built in 1897 and which stood at 11th and Central Ave, moved in 1974 to a new frame building at 30th St. and Bay Ave."

I am grateful to Bill for sharing his knowledge of this history of Ocean City's churches.

What <u>Has</u> Changed?

The Bayfront

Currently, the bayfront has very little in the way of boatyards, boat buildings, bait stores, boat rentals, gas docks, repair, and service and storage areas, compared to what it once had just a few years back. Sightseeing boat rides and restaurants on the bay just don't exist, and I understand that rental wave runners and standup paddle boards have replaced the rental row boats of former days.

It also seems like there are fewer places that are accessible to the visiting public for enjoying the bayfront experience, except for those visitors with friends who own bayfront property. Currently, the best view of the bay for visitors coming into town is when they get to the top of the 9th Street Bridge.

On the positive side, many more people actually live on the bayfront, thanks to the vast number of condo units that didn't exist before, with possibly a greater number of small private boat slips. And let's face it: Many of those former individual homes on the bay were in need of major renovation or replacement. The addition of the lagoons south of Arkansas Avenue has added many more waterfront properties and boat slips. This must be considered a positive change, certainly in the eyes of those owners.

The bottom line is that although the Ocean City waterfront is no longer the old, sleepy, slower paced lifestyle with fishing, crabbing in rental rowboats, and hanging around boat yards, people do find their own way to enjoy themselves.

Old Hotels to Motels

I always think about people of my generation—including those who are maybe 10 years older or possibly 10 years younger—who have seen the slow physical transformation of the city from the old days to the newer days. It is certainly not an exact period of time but rather a time of change in many ways.

Motels have been part of that time of change. They were not an approved use until 1959, when Al Kazmarck built the first one at 9th and Wesley Avenue. Up to that point, there were basically old hotels and old rooming houses, some of them very old. Many of the photographs and vintage postcards of these establishments, which have been published or posted on the OCNJ Chatter Facebook group page, remind me of their existence during my growing-up years and bring back many memories for me and, I bet, for you. Although many of the original hotels and rooming houses were gone before my time, I clearly remember many others before they too became the victim of the wrecking ball.

My days working as the kid at the post office gave me a unique exposure to these relics of the time, many of which were in very nice, traditional condition. The Strand, The Hanscom, The Lincoln, The Delaware, The Oceanic, The Biscayne, and of course, The Flanders, were the glue that for many years kept the city's resort industry intact. I hope I didn't forget one of your favorites.

These large hotels were outnumbered by the numerous rooming houses both large and small, as well as by the smaller hotels. In fact, I think it is fair to say that any homeowner who wanted to rent out a room or two, a second floor, or a garage apartment did so and continues to do so today, with many renting to the same families year after year.

Although the old bygone hotels were very much a signature part of the city, many of those structures have been razed to make room for newer buildings such as condos and duplexes, all of which appear to look the same, at least to me. Nevertheless, the same type of change happens everywhere, especially up and down the Jersey shore. I see it here in the Asbury Park area, where I have lived for over 55 years. Nearby Ocean Grove is probably the least-changed town on the shore, but there has definitely been change there too. However, Ocean Grove has sought to keep the look consistent with the past, with architectural standards that require traditional or Victorian design.

As for younger generations, they can only look at old photos to get a feeling of the pre-motel and pre-duplex era. In a way that is sad, but the new generations will have their own memories of life in the city. For example, on the OCNJ Chatter Facebook group, people sometimes recall life in Ocean City back in the 1980s and 1990s, which to them is nostalgic, but to me is just last week.

As for duplexes, are they really all that new? When I was growing up in Ocean City, we had many two-family homes that were first floor, second floor, but we didn't refer them as duplexes, just two-family, and many of them had been around for a long time, and many that remain have been nicely remodeled.

Alleys, What a Bright Idea

When did today's city planners, architects, and designers decide that new cities and developments would not include alleys? Fortunately, alleys were part of the original layout of Ocean City from its inception. Most of us know that our founders, the Lake brothers, laid out our alleys, and we're glad they did. After all, alleys are where you access your garage, park your car if you don't have a garage, put out your trash and recycle cans, and best of all, have a place where kids can safely play. How many basketball backboards hang off alley-adjacent garages? We had one.

Alleys also provide more street parking and a place for contractors and service people to access your home. In my childhood, those service people included the iceman and the milkman. In some cases, alleys were the only way you could access some homes on the bayfront.

Some other parts of town, like The Gardens, were laid out after the founding of the city and do not have the coveted alleys. If I'm not mistaken, Merion Park was the only newer development (if you can call the early 1950s "newer") that was laid out without alleys. Call them what you want, but to me, alleys in Ocean City were and still are an asset.

Our Italian-American Neighbors

When I was a pre-teenager, I came to realize that many of the Italian-American families in Ocean City lived on Simpson Avenue or adjacent to it. My siblings and I had many friends who lived in this neighborhood. Our friends had names like Montagna, Calise, Foglio, Miraglilo, Esposito, Ciliberto, Longo, Sannino, Taccarino, Varano, DelCorio, Annarelli, Talese, Pileggi, Palermo, Brunnetti, Trofa, Cappezza, Costello, Impagliazzo, Castaldi, Allegretto, Evangelista, and Migliaccio, just to name a few.

What I really remember as a kid is going to the Christmas party held by the Columbus Club on Simpson Avenue, off Ninth Street. Santa Claus had gifts and food for all who attended. This was an event every kid didn't want to miss.

Touring this area recently showed me that many, if not all, of the homes on Simpson Avenue that I remember from childhood have been replaced or redesigned significantly. I got over it, especially when I saw the "Macaroni Street" sign at 9th and Simpson. I must say it's pretty clever and heartwarming and pays perfect tribute to the Italian-American community, from the first arrivals to the generations that followed.

Members of this community became police officers, police chiefs, firemen, and fire chiefs. Some became city commissioners and mayors. Many local businesses, such as grocery stores or sub shops, were owned and operated by these fine families. I remember working for the Department of Public Works in the summer, along with some of my friends' fathers who were first-generation Italian-Americans. These men held onto their language, had a good work ethic that stood out, and, most important, were just flat-out good people.

This is not to say that Italian-Americans didn't have obstacles or challenges over the years; of course they did. I urge you to read *Unto The Sons* by Gay Talese, Ocean City's own most famous writer, and you will learn just what Italian-Americans faced and overcame.

The Columbus Club, which hosted the annual Christmas party we kids eagerly anticipated. Courtesy of Steve Warnalis.

Sandlot Sports

I guess I'm getting to be an old fuddy-duddy, but when I was a kid we didn't have Little League Baseball or Pop Warner Football. These organized sports came a few years later. What we normally did was get together for pickup games. This meant that a bunch of us would gather on a Saturday morning in the fall and play football on what we called the campgrounds; specifically, on the corner of 6th and Asbury Avenue. We would choose up teams and play. No helmets, pads, or anything. This was when we were maybe in the 7th or 8th grade, just before many of us got on the high school football team as freshmen. Anyhow, our pickup games, whether football or baseball, were really a lot of fun, and we all got along just great.

When baseball season came in the spring, a similar system occurred. We played in an empty lot on the southwest corner of 11th and Simpson, or behind the Surf Theater at 12th and Ocean Avenue, which at that time was just a big gravel parking lot used in the summer. Also, we would play at the real baseball field at 5th and Bay, but again, just us kids; no coaches or parents screaming at each other. How could we be so lucky?

We didn't know the term "sandlot" at the time; we just had fun. We did, however, have a small basketball program that was held at the Convention Hall at 6th and the Boardwalk. That was about it. Nick Palermo, owner of Leon's Men Shop, was our coach.

Youth basketball program. Front: Jerry Thompson. 2nd row: Gene McMurray, Phil Huber, Ken Weaver. 3rd row: Roland Claville, Dave Loder, George Sherby, Jim Jeffries. Back row: Coach Nick Palermo.

Oh, Those High School Days

When we really think back on our youth, our time and experiences in high school seem to be the first things that come to our minds. In high school, we mature rather fast and are at a stage when we make many decisions on our own. We flat-out grow up, right? Some choices are good, some not so good, and some just plain stupid. If we're lucky, at a later date, we do sometimes get a break in correcting some of our bad teenage choices.

Developing more friendships, planning for the future, becoming role models, participating in new activities, are areas that are part of high school life. At the time we don't even think about the lasting effect any of it has for our future. We were just enjoying the moment.

High school fun, from my 8th grade model club to prom night in senior year. (L) 8th grade Model Club, front row, from left to right: Gordon Lindbloom, Harry Pierce, Dave Loder, George Sherby. 2nd row: unsure, Cyril Dill, Bob Merryman, Tom Jones, Vince Evangelista. 3rd row: Jim Jeffries, Dewey Powell, Harold Gannon, Bill Blevin, John Carew. (R) Prom photo, courtesy of Ed Goldberg.

In our case, going to high school started in the 7th grade. We were exposed to the juniors and seniors who were, in some cases, idols to us. We were even allowed to join the high school band. Somehow we magically became a class with some sense of identity, our own school spirit and class spirit, as all classes do at some point. As freshmen, we noticed and observed what the classes ahead of us were doing. We got to know those students, athletes, and others. All of this is sooo... GOOD!

Another key part of our high school life was the intramural sports program, which introduced us to sports other than football, basketball, baseball, and track. These other sports included volleyball, swimming, soccer, tennis, boxing, and a little bit of gymnastics. I'm sure I've forgotten some.

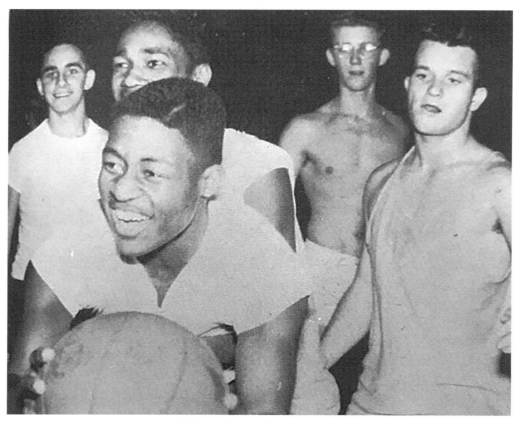

My classmates playing intramural basketball in this photo: Phil Huber, Lou Davis, Wayne Thompson, Harry Pierce, Dave Loder. Image courtesy of Ed Goldberg.

Coach Fenton Carey and Coach Dixie Howell made sure we were evenly divided up into teams. I guess the objective was that those of us who weren't considered athletic got to participate and did the best they could, which was good for everyone. The girls had a similar intramural program, which I think included badminton, tennis, swimming, field hockey, and maybe a few other sports.

Most important, in gym class we began to understand the importance of teamwork.

Without a doubt, going from Central Avenue School to OCHS was a monumental step for everyone and instrumental in preparing us for the years to follow. Even after all these years, reconnecting with fellow classmates at reunions is something that gets my juices going. We just can't help reliving those moments from 40, 50, and yes, 60 years ago.

Our high school cheerleaders, from left to right: Carol Turner Hadkte, Marla Adams, Joyce Harkins, Joan Sampson Wiegel, Joan Guarracino, Brenda Harkins, Bonnie Cunningham, Marion Swartz. Image courtesy of Ed Goldberg.

Teachers, Coaches, and Others

Although we could not have realized it at the time, I'm sure we can all agree that many teachers we had from kindergarten through 12th grade have had a lifelong impact on our lives. Many of these individuals were part of the character building phase of our youth and are the ones we think back on when we get into that nostalgia mode.

If you start thinking about this time in your life, you might be able to vividly remember a conversation you had with one of these teachers that either changed your life or pointed you in the right direction. Here's one I had that went something like this:

"You think I should call your mother, Jim?" asked my high school principal, George Meyers, as I sat in his office. I don't recall why I was sent to the office, but it was a humiliating experience. My 7th grade teacher, Mr. Pearl, was the Chief Accuser. It must have been a minor offense, as Mr. Meyers never called Mom, but he did say, "Maybe I'll mention this to your brother Bill," who was a senior at the time. Ugh.

You see, Mr. Meyers was a close friend of my father's. They were hunters and outdoorsmen and such; they were cronies. Mr. Meyers and others in this group would come to the house for Mom's famous oyster stew or her snapper soup. I often think that if it weren't for her oyster stew, I would have been treated differently by Mr. Meyers. Maybe that's a stretch, but little and sometimes silly things like this are game changers.

Then there were the coaches.

For boys in particular, phys-ed teachers and coaches seem to have a unique and mostly positive influence on us. My first phys-ed teacher was Coach T.J. Carey at

Central Avenue School, who would teach us basketball fundamentals like passing and dribbling, and even wrestling.

Many who went to Central Avenue School will recall how incredibly low the basement ceiling was at this old school. It was so low that Coach T.J. Carey could reach up and touch the basketball ring.

When I went from Central Avenue School to the high school, Coach T.J. Carey left the teaching profession to build a highly successful real estate business with his wife, Betty. The most important thing about Coach T.J. Carey is that he had such a warm and friendly personality that you just couldn't forget him.

T.J. Carey's brother Fenton Carey, along with Dixie Howell, were our coaches in high school and became exemplars of good character and mentorship. They had so much skill in getting the best out of each athlete in such a positive way, that you never forgot those invisible teaching moments.

Coach Fenton Carey was known never to use swear words or, as he referred to them, "cuss words," and I'll never forget the time he talked to us about that subject. His reasoning was this: "If you have to use cuss words, it just shows your ignorance of the English language."

This advice was hard to argue with and something that stuck with me and others. Coach Fenton Carey also had little patience for those he caught smoking or those whom he heard were smoking. There was always the possibility of being thrown off the team if caught. Fortunately, I didn't have to worry about that; as I mentioned before, I quit when I was 11.

(L to R) Our high school principal, George Meyers. Unforgettable Coach Fenton Carey.
Ralph Jarvis, beloved English teacher. Courtesy of Ed Goldberg.

Then there's Ralph Jarvis, my high school English teacher. He is high on my list, and I'm sure that is true for other former students as well. Mr. Jarvis had the ability to get your attention in many ways, sometimes with dry humor, which didn't always register with some.

In my case, and that of my older siblings, we had a more personal relationship with this icon, because he and his wife, Carrie, were very close friends with our mother. We also went to the same church, and Mr. Jarvis sang in the choir. He was a good singer and knew his church music. Mr. Jarvis and Mom were also active in the Eastern Star, which is some Masonic Lodge type organization, and were "Matron and Patron" the same year, whatever that means.

In addition, Mr. Jarvis worked summers at the post office, riding his bike from home to be a window clerk selling postal money orders and special deliveries. I'm sure he got the job from Pop, the postmaster. What's the word, nepotism? Or is it who you know? Either way, kudos to a family friend and teacher who meant a lot to me and others, a man born and raised in Oklahoma.

Here's my final and favorite Mr. Jarvis story.

Many years after he retired, Mr. Jarvis and his wife lived up in the Cape Cod area near where their son lived. Mr. Jarvis may have been 90 years old or so when my wife, Kathy, and I paid him a surprise visit one summer day. I knocked on the door, and when he opened it, I said, "Hi, I'm Jim Jeffries."

Without a pause, he quickly and loudly said, "OF COURSE YOU ARE!"

Typical Ralph Jarvis; not one to be upstaged.

I don't recall ever having had any young teachers. They were all OLD. I mean for the entire K through 12 experience. Of course, if one were 30, that would be old to a kid.

Then there are the little things that mean a lot; for instance, when my 5th-grade teacher, Miss Ogden, made my day. It happened when she wrote on the blackboard on the last day of the school year: "NEVER—ABSENT—NEVER LATE—Jimmy Jeffries." I was up there with the straight-A students, for the first and last time. I later learned that Miss Ogden lived to be around 103 years of age. I attribute that longevity to simply being a nice person to all of us who went to Central Avenue School.

State Champs

Without question, the highlight of my years at OCHS was when we won the Group 1 New Jersey State Basketball Championship in 1955, and I was on the team. Some may not remember that, but I was the "manager," and my name is on the huge trophy presented to the team, along with Captain Frank Wickes, Joe Kennedy, Chick McDowell, Phil Huber, Harry Hoff, Teddy Ford, Nate Davis, Sam Foglio, Bernie Carter, Wayne Hudson, Tom Adams, George Loder, and Mike Verano. Actually, my basketball skills were below zero, which is why I was asked by Coach Dixie Howell to be the one who kept score, take care of equipment, clean up after practice, and any other tasks Dixie needed done.

The high school, as well as the entire city and surrounding towns whose kids attended our school, have never been on such a high as we all were when we beat North Arlington for the State Championship, which happened to be the first state championship ever won by OCHS. Go Team Go!

Rock 'N' Roll And Fins

Who would have ever thought that the music of the 50s would still be popular 60-plus years later? Let's be honest; that era has long legs. Now it's oldies but goodies on the radio, at weddings, and it's still going strong.

Many of us who grew up in the 40s and 50s were also witnesses to our older siblings playing 78 records, those big-format vinyl records from the war era that featured artists like Sammy Kaye, Ellington, Bing Crosby, and Spike Jones. Soon after, the arrival of what we now know as rock 'n' roll took over our lives and played on the "new" 45 records.

The history of rock 'n' roll is all over the place. All we knew is that we liked it. We sang the songs, we danced, and we jitterbugged to the music, whether it was slow or fast. There were so many groups as well as solo singers formed in such a short time that we couldn't keep up with their names and newly released songs; at least I couldn't.

Out with the 78s and in with the 45s. No matter what the format, rock 'n' roll is here to stay.

Our hangouts kept us rocking and rolling. There were Mom & Pop's, The Chatterbox, The Boxwood, The Youth Center, or in the summer, the Convention Hall; and anywhere else there was a juke box, like The Point Diner. We had no idea of the magnitude of the impact these special years would have on us and the entire nation in such a short time.

Most of us were too young to go to Somers Point bars like Bay Shores, Tony Mart's, and Steele's, where bands playing this new era of music shook the entire area. These places were issued violations for allowing underage drinking in the summer, but their penalty wasn't imposed until after Labor Day, which was when they were closed. What a joke that was.

The summer traffic between Somers Point and Ocean City was legendary. Working college students, lifeguards, and just about anybody would do whatever they could to get into bars to hear the live rock 'n' roll band music. Hitchhiking was a common way of getting over the two miles of causeway.

We now know that Wildwood, New Jersey, another resort town south of Ocean City, played a part in the beginning of this new musical era. Don't believe me? Read on.

This Tony Mart's ad for a Bill Haley and the Comets concert in neighboring Somers Point brings back memories of that rock 'n' roll summer of 1956.

The connection is Bill Haley of Bill Haley and The Comets, and Dick Richards, later a resident of Ocean City. (I never met Dick Richards when he lived in Ocean City, but I'm sure some of you did.) Richards grew up in West Chester, Pennsylvania; Haley also grew up outside of Philly. Haley was putting his band together down in Wildwood, and Richards became his first drummer for the first two years of the group.

"Rock Around the Clock" and "Shake Rattle and Roll," which were two of their early hits, are recognized as being songs from the beginning of the rock 'n' roll era. I clearly remember Bill Haley and his band performing these songs in Ocean City in the summer of 1956 at Convention Hall. Our founding fathers must have been turning over in their graves.

I urge all to look up Bill Haley or Dick Richards on the internet. Unbelievable information on both of them that will make you smile.

Now, What Do "Fins" Have To Do With Rock 'n' Roll?

Actually nothing, except for the new design of cars with fins and the entry of rock 'n' roll into the music scene, both of which seemed to happen around the same time. During this era, virtually all car manufacturers created fins on the rear fenders of their new cars. This new design was almost as revolutionary as rock 'n' roll itself.

Today, seeing old photos of this time period that include both of these phenomenal but different creations brings back many memories. Local dealer showrooms greeted the curious who came to see these futuristic spaceships on wheels. It seemed that automakers were trying to out-fin each other by giving the next year's model a little larger fin.

Rock 'n' roll and fins just seemed to go together, but who knew that at the time, and who would have guessed that these cars would become collector's items years later. You can still see these restored beauties at car shows or just being driven around by their proud owners, who most likely paid ten times their original cost.

If you're from my era, I trust you recall the 1950s' dramatic change of automobile design, as I do. If not, here is a photo to stir up your memories.

Fins made you feel like you were driving a rocket ship. Photo by Clem Onojeghuo on Unsplash.

America, Here We Come

I don't know if it is true, but I once heard it said that people who grow up in Ocean City "have sand in their shoes."

I think it was my sister who told me this. Whether this is an old adage or not, it makes you think about the hidden meaning, which I always viewed this way: You're born here, you live here, and you die here.

This is of course not always the case, but as young people we didn't consider such things. We were just living our childhood to the hilt and weren't thinking beyond the 9th Street Bridge.

When we were rather young, our idea of "out of town" could be no more than a 15-mile radius. Sure, we may have gone to Somers Point, Atlantic City, or even Philadelphia on occasion. And if you were a kid involved in varsity sports, it took you to towns like Hammonton or Cape May. But we didn't think about traveling much farther than that because we "love every inch of our soil," as the song about Ocean City states. We were having too much fun right here, thank you very much.

At some point in our lives, we begin to think about our future. Reality lingers in our heads, and our future plans, dreams, and ideas do not always include the town we grew up in. This realization comes to light for different people at different times, but surely it's a life-changing period for many. Some of us had no idea what or where our future would be; I certainly didn't.

I never asked myself the question of what I was going to do after high school. I wasn't prepared for college and never thought I could ever make it academically, though some of my classmates proved, later on, that they could do it.

Mr. Henriod, our guidance counselor, convinced me to go to a two-year program at Peirce Business School in Philadelphia. Four days after I graduated from high school, my father died, and we had little if any money to spare, but I finally did end up commuting to Philly every day by train to attend this school.

As a result, I got to know the big city some and was exposed to businesses that were bigger than Stainton's Department Store and Ocean City National Bank. Somehow the sand gets out of your shoes, one grain at a time, and you begin to see a new world. Many of you had a similar experience when at college, at Fort Dix, or somewhere else beyond the 9th Street Bridge.

Sure, many classmates went on to college and became teachers, doctors, and engineers, never to return except for visits. Others simply got a job and went to work or joined the military; I think Dave Loder and Jerry Platt were in the army immediately after graduation. Others joined the municipal work force as firemen, policemen, and other city workers. For the most part, our industry was seasonal, and remains so to this day.

It is not like some flash of light from the heavens, but we learn there is life outside our beloved town. Suddenly, we are no longer kids growing up between the bay and the beach. Opportunity becomes a driving force in our young lives, and we may find ourselves somewhere miles away.

Destiny simply shows us the way, subliminally or otherwise, to America as we know it today. Whether destiny keeps us in Ocean City for life or takes us to California, we never, ever forget our roots that will always remain in Ocean City. We never forget the people who were such a positive force in molding our character, and who did not forget us.

We could compare the migration of those of us who left Ocean City for other parts of America, to our forefathers who flocked to an island once called Peck's Beach on the Jersey Shore, the island that would, in 1879, become Ocean City, New Jersey. The city needed builders, laborers, masons, real estate people, architects, fisherman, livery stables, transportation, hoteliers, rooming house owners, and merchants to serve the growing population and the influx of thousands in the summer. Back then, almost all the young people in Ocean City remained there until their dying day and with sand in their shoes. The stampede to the Jersey Shore during the mid 1800's was akin to the Gold Rush to California.

Up and down the entire Jersey Shore, from Cape May to Sandy Hook, other towns were being established and built around the same time as Ocean City. Today, this skinny stretch of 125 miles of beach, sand dunes, boardwalks, bays, roads, causeways, and bridges collectively draws millions each and every year. Someday the Jersey Shore will become a "Wonder of the World," but I'm not sure what number it will receive.

Nevertheless, many of us natives of Ocean City needed or were somehow required to find a new life and future somewhere other than our hometown. By design, planning, destiny, or dumb luck, we somehow managed to find our new Shangri-La, a place as good as our hometown, a place where our kids could grow up.

I was fortunate that my new Ocean City became Asbury Park, New Jersey and the surrounding area. Though only 85 miles north of Ocean City, at times it felt like 1,000 miles, and I didn't get back home as much as I should have.

Mom passed in 1969 at 69; my brother, Bill, died at home in 1993 at 59; and my sister, Annetta, died in 2011 at 80. I have one remaining second cousin still living in Ocean City.

Fortunately, new families with new names from other places now call Ocean City home. And the beat goes on.

Save your memories!

The last day I lived in Ocean City was April 25, 1959. I was only 20 years of age. It took me nearly 61 years to fully realize that I should express my love for my hometown, Ocean City, New Jersey, and to share some memories, with you.

May Ocean City never change, but I know it will, and for the better.

My brother, Bill, on the left; and me, on my wedding day in 1959. This is when I said goodbye to my Ocean City life and embarked on a new and exciting journey with my wife, Kathy.

Social Media

To discover more about Ocean City in the 40s and 50s and other bygone decades, and to share your own memories, consider participating in the Facebook groups OCNJ Chatter and Ocean City, NJ History and Memories. This platform for sharing photos, stories, and just about anything Ocean City provides me with an opportunity to feel like I still live there today. I chime in when I feel I have something to offer.

Often, I recognize a familiar name or a family name and have connected with some old neighbors, friends, their children, grandchildren, and others via these sites. Hats off to those that keep this going and to all those who contribute with stories, comments, photos, and questions.

Google Earth

If you really want to get a modern view of Ocean City, I highly recommend Google Earth, which you can visit on your web browser at www.google.com/earth/. You can also download the app on your computer, phone, iPad, or other tablet. If you have trouble doing this, ask your grandson for help.

Under "search," type in any Ocean City, New Jersey address, or just type in "Ocean City, NJ." From there you can move around anywhere you want to have a bird's eye view of the city. You can find your house and neighborhood, or anything else if it still exists.

There are several fun options that you can play with on this app. You will be surprised at the detail. It makes you feel like an eagle, or in our case, a sea gull.

Too bad this app can't show what the city looked like many years ago. Now that would be fantastic. In any case, it is great fun and a bit addictive. You can go anywhere in the world.

Many Thanks

Shortly after I started writing these accounts, I learned about the two Facebook groups I've referred to throughout this book, Ocean City, NJ History & Memories and OCNJ Chatter. It took me about 10 seconds to sign up and become a member. I can't begin to tell you what a resource these chat rooms and friends have been to me. Not just a resource, but total enjoyment as a participant. I found old friends and made new ones, and I thank you all for supporting me on this journey. Ken Tillotson, the admin for both groups, is <u>The Man</u> on this one. Keep it growing, Ken!

If you, dear reader, are not a member and you love Ocean City, I urge you to sign up now:

www.facebook.com/groups/OceanCityNJChatter/

www.facebook.com/groups/OceanCityNJHistoryandMemories/

If you are a descendant of any of Ocean City's early residents, please document and share your family's history in Ocean City with these groups, because preserving history is important, and all of us who love Ocean City would love to know more about its history.

I want to particularly thank Steve Warnalis; Ken Tillotson; Bill Pehlert, a volunteer at the Ocean City Historical Museum; Rahn Brackin; Fred Miller; Steve Gring; George Loder; Nate Davis; Ed May; Herb Godfrey; ALL those who have assisted me with obtaining information and photographs; my book designer, Mehran "Ronnie" Azma; and of course my editor, Laurie Rigler.

Special thanks to my wife, Kathy, for her solid support; my daughter, Brenda; and my grandson, Dan Skinner, my remote IT guy who saved me many times. That's what grandsons are supposed to do.

Thanks to the following friends who shared with me their fondest memories of their growing-up years in Ocean City:

"As little kids, my brother Frank, Bill Cox and I would go to the 4th St. Train Station and offer to carry the suitcases for the arriving passengers. Sometimes it was only to an awaiting car and sometimes it was several blocks away. To receive a quarter or some small amount was very important to us. It was a job, and we learned how important it was to treat visitors well."
—George Wickes, Class of 1957

"I was a student at St Augustine's School at 2nd & Atlantic during World War II. We had piles of metal in our playground. This was part of the city-wide collection of material to support the war effort. I also remember Navy training planes over the beach with live ammunition, shooting at targets being towed by other planes. Sometimes the empty shells landed on the beach."
—Pat Henry, Age 83, retired fireman

"We lived over Essig's Restaurant at 9th & Asbury Ave. My father was a fireman at the 6th Street Firehouse. Mother would make his dinner and I would take it to the firehouse in a wicker basket. My neighbors were the Lee family that owned the laundry a couple of doors away. They tried but failed to teach me how to use chopsticks. Wasn't I lucky to live in such an innocent time?"
—Marlene Moncrief Murphy, Class of 1957

"My best friend in grade school was Evan Kimball, who lived on the bay in 'The Gardens.' Evan would have the family chauffeur stop and pick me up at 312 West Avenue, a dirt street at the time, and take us to Central Avenue School. After the 6th grade, he was sent to a private school but we remained good friends. This is one of my fondest memories from my young days in Ocean City."
—Nate Davis, Class of 1955

"I have a thousand great memories of Ocean City. My two personal favorites are, my father taking me up into 'The Tower' on top of the Music Pier, during the war where they looked for enemy submarines. The other was going to the A&P with my mother on 8th Street and using wartime ration stamps that were blue/red ration tokens. Glory Days."
—Marla Adams, Class of 1956

Thanks for taking this trip back in time with me.

About The Author

J im Jeffries' community-minded spirit extends beyond his beloved birthplace of Ocean City. A longtime resident of the Asbury Park area of New Jersey, Jim was for many years active in his local Chamber of Commerce, Board of Education, and The Rotary Club. He also served as President of the New Jersey Jaycees.

Along with these grown-up responsibilities, Jim is also, in many ways, still the kid he was in the 1940s and 50s. Voted "Class Wit" in high school, he has maintained that reputation by doing a number of roasts for friends and others at private events. He even got paid for one of them.

Today, having retired from a long and successful career as a State Farm Insurance agent, Jim happily writes, golfs, and plans the next adventure. He and his wife, Kathy, who will forever be the girl he married all those years ago, split their time between Palm Beach Gardens, Florida and their home in New Jersey.

Made in the USA
Middletown, DE
17 January 2021